ABOVE AND BEYOND

HOW TO BUILD IMPACTFUL BUSINESSES

WHERE EVERYBODY WINS!

R. SRINIVASAN
SHRIHARI UDUPA
R. MUKUND

SPOTLIGHT
by notionpress.com

Old No. 38, New No. 6
McNichols Road, Chetpet
Chennai - 600 031

First Published by Notion Press 2020
Copyright © R. Srinivasan, Shrihari Udupa, R. Mukund 2020
All Rights Reserved.

ISBN

Hardcase: 978-1-64733-554-0
Paperback: 978-1-64850-868-4

Contents

Testimonials

....

"Very timely in our current restless, conflicted, chaotic, unstable, divided and confusing world.

It seems that many organizations have young, smart people who learn fast, move quickly and succeed and then lose momentum. These concepts could give them what they need… to keep their people and move into a whole new realm of success.

I actually scanned the book by studying the great graphics, read the personal stories, with that overview, I then came back and read straight through. Quite enjoyable"

– Gail West
ICA Taiwan

* * * *

The term, "impactful business" is tossed around in organizations every now and then, risking the loss of its in-depth meaning. The definition of "impactful business" generally gets modified and interpreted by organizations to suit their culture and the end goals. The attempts made towards creating an impact are not always enough as the physicists point out that even the beat of a tiny butterfly's wing creates an impact. The success recipe is to take steps in order to make more conscious and an intentional impact and, subsequently, support the ecosystem to reach a larger or a higher purpose.

This book meticulously focuses on the depth of an approach to be adopted to drive change and create the desired impact. The holistic and pragmatic framework suggested by the authors is truly based on experiential learning and resonates with the pace of this ever-changing world we live in. The book takes us through the subtle nuances of a spectrum of themes that are a prerequisite to creating meaningful impact. The authors deserve compliments for the parameters identified and dissected via the medium of this book which, I am sure, will help the readers demystify the art of creating an impact in their pursuits.

Best wishes

– Kamal Bali
President & Managing Director, Volvo Group – India

* * * *

Well researched, prolifically anecdotal, philosophically laced with living examples of people, Organisations and situations, these three practicing Manager-Authors bring you a book with a different ending…An ending which keeps you going 'above and beyond'… An ending which seeks to ensure that everyone lives happily ever after.

Written in a breezy easy-to-read style, this study is actually deep, insightful and thought-provoking. By rightly bringing in a

4th P – PURPOSE – to Profit, People and Planet, the Authors have highlighted the pressing urgency of sustainability. Remember, a Company's Purpose needs to address who it is today and who it wants to be tomorrow. And without a solid, convincing purpose, no Company can transform itself.

If achieving excellence and success are asymptotic phenomena, going beyond excellence on the path of sustained lasting success is a life-long pursuit in seeking the very purpose of an impactful Organisation and linking it with its *raison d'etre*, its Purpose, whilst simultaneously nurturing Teams of motivated, inspired, self-fulfilled People whose own purpose resonates with the Organisation's Purpose.

In our mission to sustainably go 'above and beyond', the Authors beautifully weave in the *vedantic* message of a **Larger Purpose** – a "Higher Cause" that encompasses a **Holistic Vision** and values that inspire People to the *mantra* of *seva bhava* (selfless service), delighting the customer's customer and making a difference, with no expectation of return, but with immense, innate gratitude for being able to perform that *seva*.

Above and Beyond deftly completes the virtuous cycle of how impactful Organisations knit their Purpose with People to deliver sustainably and profitably to the Planet.

– Pradeep Mallick
former MD, Wartsila India;
now an executive coach and independent director.

* * * *

The book "Above And Beyond" written by highly accomplished and experienced practising professionals is a very timely reminder of what is truly at the core of any business.

One has long heard the heard the paradigm, "Culture eats Strategy for breakfast" but one has also seen that over the last two decades or so the extreme focus on short term financial performance Coupled with unrealistic "valuations" has resulted in a completely distorted behaviour pattern among business leaders and employees. We have almost made employees into schizophrenics who follow one set of values from 9 to 5 in the office and another set of values from 5 to 9 at home. The book explains how Culture is developed and sustained over long periods of time. The book is almost like a manual that covers organisations in all stages of development and suggests a detailed step by step approach that are easy for any manager to follow.

The book brilliantly brings home the point that business is ultimately about making a difference to society that society is all about people. Businesses can be huge drivers of social change which in turn can be only achieved if the employees see themselves as agents of change.

The simplicity of language and multitude of real life examples coming brings home the point in a vivid and easy way.

I would highly recommend this book to not only practising managers but also for business schools and young students. I compliment the authors in having condensed their years of experience into easy to understand and practical wisdom.

– Banmali Agrawala
President - Infrastructure and Defence & Aerospace,
Tata Sons Private Limited

* * * *

I agree with what the book endorses that "Human being does not live for only bread alone but **Larger Purpose**". Even Materials have a soul, and so do human beings. Human being are not just to be merely there, but be meaningful. Humans are irreplaceable in heaven and earth. That is our pride.

This book is not only Widia Story but also has elements of "Human Drama" which every mankind will use to change their lives. We can notice that in Japan, we have our own "**Larger Purpose**" encompassing respect, trust and love for each other.

Indians and Japanese may be alike in basic human values through dharma, pride and contribution to larger good.

– Teruhiko Masuda
Ex President – MMC
(Mitsubishi Materials Japan) & Mitsubishi Hitachi
Tools Japan.

* * * *

This is a must-read book for those wanting to build and grow sustainable organisations in the uncertain times we live in. I have known R Srinivasan and Widia for several decades. Both stand out for their focus on and commitment to excellence and are beacons not only for their industry but for the manufacturing world at large. The book is replete with relatable examples and conceptual frameworks thus providing today's leaders with a ready-to-use toolkit to create truly impactful organisations.

– Hema Hattangady
Independent Director, Thought leader,
Ex CEO – Conserve Systems (Part of Schneider Electric)

* * * *

Over my years of business leadership, of executive coaching, of executive teaching and of entrepreneurship, I came to realise that offering purposeful situations to people, society, clients and owners was paramount to ensure business success, in the short and longer terms, irrespective of the current political, economic or social context.

Putting together their business experience with academic perspective, the authors of this book, R. Srinivasan, Shrihari Udupa and R. Mukund, offer a practical guide for business leaders who dare to transform their company to respond to the need for Purpose, and for start-ups who want to lay down the foundations of their business in the most effective and lasting manner.

From big picture conversations to detailed decisions, from culture and leadership to recruitment and development, 'Above and Beyond' covers all aspects that business leaders need to address to ensure their company becomes an impactful organisation. An organization fit for the 21st century.

– Stephane Lhuillier
Executive coach, Associate professor, Entrepreneur
Paris, France

* * * *

Foreword

....

How do business organizations live for long and stay ahead of the competition in the onslaught of myriad changes happening in the environment? This is a question that continues to baffle serious researchers and practitioners in the domain of business. Several books and theories have been proposed to address this issue. One paradigm is that the goal of an organization is to make profit. Several have also proposed the critical role of leadership and strategic thinking. Against this backdrop it was indeed a pleasant task to go through the book, *Above and Beyond,* which brings fresh perspectives to address this important question.

The book stands out on three counts; First, it brings out a rich experience of Shri R. Srinivasan and two other industry experts of living through this fundamental question and navigating a business organization in its journey through a brick-by-brick building approach. Second, there is a very careful and well thought out blend of concepts and real-life stories. Moreover, appropriate use of schematic sketches to communicate these ideas have made it easy to understand the subtle concepts presented. These delicate choices have made the entire material a pleasure to go through.

Third, it has, from the very beginning, taken a fresh perspective to the possible initiatives that an organization can take to stay relevant and successful for a long time. For instance, while it is customary to talk about the role of values, in this book they have taken a deep dive approach in dissecting the notion of values and spanning them across holistic human values, dharmic values, business ethics and operating values. Such an approach to discuss the ideas presented has enabled the authors to bring new perspectives to the problem and the possible solutions.

The ideas presented in the book challenges some of the fundamental notions that we hold about certain aspects of managing a business organisation. For instance, if we carefully analyse our practices and assumptions, we will notice that we treat human beings as one more type of resource that an organization can make use of. However, the book brings out the unique features of human beings as a key resource that cares deeply for "meaning making".

In the context of this basic attribute of a human being, the book presents the dichotomy between individual and organization and seeks to provide a unifying framework to harmoniously address this dichotomy. In fact, the book presents this inevitable dichotomous situation in an organization and builds several new ideas to address this dichotomy instead of blissfully being ignorant of this or pushing this issue under the carpet. The book makes a bold claim that the ability of the leader to develop synergy between organisational purpose and meaning making at an individual level is crucial to building world class organisations of the future.

The other insightful contribution of this book is a wholesome and a new approach to the issue of building "value driven" organisation. The notion of value is generally narrowly defined, pertaining to certain practices and etiquettes. In such an approach, the attempt is to somehow link it with the culture of an organisation.

On the contrary, in this book, the authors have taken steps to bring out a wide gamut of issues that indeed shape the value. They have been able to beautifully blend some of the indigenous dharmic practices into the discussion. This has the potential to enrich our own understanding of the notion of value and its importance in building outstanding business organizations.

This book offers enough food for thought for inspirational leaders, who want to make a difference to themselves, and to the society at large by investing significant efforts in building a lasting and a great organization. The joy of leaving such a legacy is known only to a few and such people will find an ideal companion in this book to shape their thoughts and channelize their efforts.

It is indeed my privilege and pleasure to share my thoughts on *Above and Beyond*. I wish the authors the very best and earnestly hope that they will see the fruits of their efforts by way of witnessing welcome changes in the manner some of us will lead business organisations in the future.

– B Mahadevan
Professor of Operations Management
Indian Institute of Management Bangalore
(Formerly Vice Chancellor,
Chinmaya Vishwavidyapeeth, Ernakulam)
http://www.iimb.ac.in/webpages/b-mahadevan

PREFACE

Impact
Transcending Business

· ·

Today, more than ever before, there is a sharp dichotomy between the goals of an organisation and its employees. This lack of synergy in focus between employee goals and company goals is at the root of a lot of conflict and frustration, manifesting in trends such as frequent job switches, higher burn out rates and abandoning of careers midway to do something completely different. At all levels across ages, people seem to be grappling with a difficult question—of finding meaning in what they do. The organisations in turn struggle with a churn in people, lack of stability and face great difficulty in having stable operations to achieve their business objectives.

Business goals are usually focused on the three Ps—of Profits, (and to a lesser extent) People and the Planet. Often, the creation of shareholder wealth overrides all other concerns, including people. This only reinforces the feeling of dissatisfaction and lack of meaning.

This book attempts to define success and link it to a *purpose** in business and work life.

---

*   Words marked * are used with a specific meaning in the context of this book. Please see Glossary for explanation.

How much of success comes from business strategies, innovations, technologies and acquisitions?

Is there anything beyond this kind of success*?

How important is the role of the leader in determining the success of the organisation and the people?

And finally, what truly takes organisations to a stage of impactful and lasting success?

The authors propose a new personality and role for business organisations, breaking away from the stereotypical perception of corporate entities as cold, calculating and purely profit focused. They believe that organisations, like people, are looking for a *Larger* Purpose. Those that adopt a spirit of serving the common good are the ones that reach beyond success and excellence to a higher, ideal state.

The book explores the idea that the growth of a company is inextricably linked with individual growth. Companies that create a culture where their people thrive are the ones that have the potential to go beyond excellence, both in terms of profit and sustainability—what we call *The Impactful Organisation.**

Organisations that go beyond excellence to become **The Impactful Organisation** typically:

- Are respected, admired and trusted by stakeholders.

- Ignite greatness in people by ensuring that they are aligned with the organisation, brimming with energy and are self-directed.

- Renew themselves and grow in a sustained manner, independent of people at the helm.

The book deals with the concepts that **The Impactful Organisation** needs to incorporate to rise beyond the current paradigms in business. These are:

- *Larger* Purpose*

- *Holistic* Values*

- *Holistic* Vision*

- *Psychic* Safety* to people

- *Nourishing* Culture*

Impactful organisations need to have a *Holistic* Vision, which embraces a *Larger* Purpose. Answering the question of *why* they exist and *how* they can serve the common good can help them identify their *Comprehensive* Vision and their *Larger* Purpose.

Clearly articulating and following a set of *Holistic* Values—beyond business ethics—can create an energetic and effervescent workplace that allows people to operate without contradictions and conflicts. To achieve this kind of energetic engagement of people, the leadership needs to put in thought and effort into nurturing its people and providing the right kind of *Psychic* Safety.

Drawing on the collective experience of the authors, the book offers an interesting perspective of both people and organisations. The book contains stories that illustrate the Widia culture and the little things that made it stand out among others in the industry. And how that kind of thinking continues to the impact the professional and personal lives and of ex-Widians even decades later.

The company that rose to the position of market leadership and continues to lead even today has spawned an enviable 200+ CEOs, heads of organisations and successful entrepreneurs—all of whom believed in Widia's core belief of nurturing people and helping them align their lives to a *Larger* **Purpose**. The book stresses the importance of transcending the leader paradigm from **business only** to **business plus people**.

The authors believe that this book can provoke thought and spur ideas among young leaders, aspiring CEOs, founders of startups, managers, students of management and academic researchers in management studies.

IMPACT transcending BUSINESS

The insights into managing organisations in the corporate world are based on the authors' experience. The authors spent long years between 1970–1995 in Widia, and over the next 20 years, they have been associated with over 200+ corporates and CEOs in fields ranging from capital goods, industrial consumables, consumer products, automotive supply chain to general engineering and service industries. The authors have helped over 200,000 people tap into their potential and excel in their professional and personal lives.

Acknowledgements

With the limited experiences every individual has, it has never been possible for mortal humans to decode life in its entirety or the ways of the world. Nonetheless, trying to understand, make sense of life and decipher principles that have worked is a constant endeavour. Civilisations and generations have benefited by such efforts. This book is one such attempt. We would, therefore, like to acknowledge and express our gratitude to all those who have contributed and enabled us to gain the insights shared in this book.

Nearly two decades after going our separate ways, a thought occurred to some of us that it might be good for some old Widia colleagues to meet up. What began as a small group grew to 75, with more wanting to join. Colleagues from all corners of the country joined for the evening get together along with their spouses. This was in June 2014. The warmth, camaraderie and the energy in the air got spirits soaring. The thrill of rebonding was palpable. By then, most people had had substantial experience with other corporates post their Widia stint. Interestingly, the group was unanimous in its declaration that the Widia era in their lives was the best. It was different, unique and not found anywhere else.

That meeting set some of us—M. S. Krishnan, V. Aswatha Ramaiah, P. R. Mujumdar, R. Srinivasan, R. Mukund, S. M. Udupa—on a quest to explore and understand what made Widia experience so special and magical.

The team approached Late Dr. K.B. Akhilesh, Dean, Indian Institute of Science, Bangalore to get an impartial view. Was there something deeper to the sentiments expressed at the reunion? And if so, what was the best way to unearth the source of the magic? Dr. K.B. Akhilesh was all encouragement. He suggested that we check for feedback from a larger cross-section of ex-Widians and guided us on the way forward.

The team worked relentlessly to get Widia folks together, listen to their experiences and quiz them on the difference Widia made to their lives.

In the three meetings that were organised, the responses of around 150-odd participants indicated that Widia meant and provided different things to each of them, all diverse and enriching. Most of the respondents were ex-employees/retirees across levels and departments. The stories they shared, in a way, laid the foundation for the book and contributed to the development of the concepts enunciated. The enthusiasm and spontaneity with which people came forward to share their experiences and learnings was a very humbling experience. Our heartfelt thanks to the participants of Widia community for wholeheartedly supporting the initiative.

After capturing the perspectives of the larger group, Late Dr. K.B. Akhilesh extended further support through a post-doc researcher, through Dr. Amritha M.A., who is currently a Professor at MS Ramaiah Institute of Management and Nithin Raju, a PG Research Associate, and entrepreneur, to transcribe and analyse the inputs from the Widia colleagues.

The output only got us more excited and made our quest more determined. We will always be indebted to Dr. K.B. Akhilesh for his timely encouragement, deep involvement and guidance. His perspectives on the analysis prodded us to continue our quest, navigate and discover the hidden principles and truths. We are immensely grateful to Dr. K.B. Akhilesh, Dr. Amritha M.A. and Nithin Raju for their support and contributions.

Widia gave us the privilege of interacting with multiple stakeholders. Every situation and interaction has contributed to our understanding of what worked and what did not. This was the core of our experience, which shaped our thoughts and actions. The only way to thank everyone is by cherishing our association with them in our hearts.

Colleagues from Widia—who have moved on to other corporates or turned entrepreneurs—have contributed to the insights. By continuing to live the values, practising the learnings, making a profound impact in their subsequent assignments and inspiring and developing other leaders, they were a constant source of inspiration to us. We thank them for being torchbearers of the Widia culture and keeping it alive.

With the analysis provided by the IISc team, we tried to analyse what it was in the Widia crucible that created the chemistry and the magic. R. B. Watson, a Widia veteran, volunteered to participate during one of the many daylong deliberations. He joined as a toolmaker in the 60s and retired as the Vice President Manufacturing in the new millennium. He shared perspectives of his lifelong association of almost four decades, what Widia had offered to him and the employees and what made the difference for him. Watson provided us with a dispassionate and objective view of the Widia offerings. Thanks, R. B. Watson, for your passionate belief in Widia and its culture.

We cherish the enthusiastic participation of M.S. Krishnan, P. R. Majumdar and V. Aswatha Ramaiah in organising the multiple meetings and collecting experiences from various members of the Widia staff. Their insights and analysis of the stories have been extremely valuable. We thank each of them for their unstinted support and contributions to the quest.

A doubt that nagged us continuously was whether the concepts propounded would contribute to the knowledge base and their utility to the current corporate community. Our anxieties were set to rest by Dr. B. Mahadevan, Professor at the Indian Institute of Management, Bangalore. After a patient hearing, he provided adequate endorsement of our ideas by sharing international perspectives and the latest research with us. It was music to our ears when he validated the idea of dharma, larger good and the spirit of service in a corporate context. Our gratitude and pranaams to Dr. Mahadevan for enabling the final leap.

Given that the manuscript was tedious, there was a need to make the content simple, clear and crisp. We were lucky to quickly discover Ms. Chitra Phadnis. She was really quick to understand what is perceived as theoretical, 'soft' stuff in business and simplify it. Our deep appreciation and thanks to Chitra for her total commitment to uncomplicate the complex propositions.

Given the novices we were, the publication of the book was the next challenge. It was sheer serendipity that brought us, during our explorations, to the doorsteps of Notion Press in Chennai. The enthusiasm, energy and speed of the Notion Press teams were extremely contagious; we did not feel the need to go or check out elsewhere. Only people who are propelled by a purpose can manage to attain their goals. Notion Press reflected the spirit of everything that we were trying to say in the book. The wholehearted involvement and commitment of the team in making the book a reality has been commendable. A big 'thank you' to the Notion Press team.

It would be unfair if we do not acknowledge the tolerance of idiosyncrasies, patience reflected and unstinted support provided by our spouses Vatsala Srinivasan, Anuradha Udupa and Gayathri Mukund. Our deepest gratitude, appreciation and heartfelt thanks to them.

Last but not the least, we need to thank the Almighty and the creators of the opportunity and platform called Widia, which brought together great people and enabled the wonderful journey to make meaningful contributions. Hopefully, with the offering of this book, we have repaid a small portion of our debts.

About the Authors

R. Srinivasan

R. Srinivasan, popularly called "Guru", played a lead role in setting up Widia (India) Ltd. and nurturing its growth into a well-respected and admired organisation between the years 1966 to 1994.

Under his leadership, Widia (India) became an incubation centre of sorts for new leaders. Widia has the distinction of having created over 200 CEOs, entrepreneurs and domain leaders.

After his long stint as Managing Director of Widia (India) Ltd., R. Srinivasan (RS) has been an adviser and mentored more than 25 organisations, helping them put together a vision and chalk out strategies for sustained progress. He has also been on the board of at least 20 organisations including Tube Investments and Mindtree Ltd. He continues to be on the Board of Sundaram Fasteners Ltd., Kirloskar Oil Engines Ltd., and TTK Prestige Ltd., as an Independent Director.

As a mentor and coach for over 100 'C suite' level executives, he has guided over 500 young leaders formally and informally to find their own true potential. He has been the President of BCIC

(Bangalore Chamber of Industries and Commerce) and Chairman of Confederation of Indian Industries (CII-KR). He was actively involved with the quality initiatives of CII and, as a senior assessor, assessed companies like TATA Steel, Infosys, TATA Motors, and Birla Carbon Thailand for Excellence in Business. He has also been a Member of the Jury for Business Excellence for the CII–Exim Business Excellence Award. As a past President of Indian Machine Tool Manufacturers Association, he continues to play an active part in developing the Indian Machine Tool Industry's growth and competitiveness.

He is a mechanical engineer from Anna University. He can be contacted at rsri126@gmail.com

Shrihari Udupa

Shrihari Udupa is an accomplished HR professional, currently associated with a not-for-profit institution, Ashoka Trust for Research in Ecology and the Environment (ATREE). He is also a Trustee at Trust for Development Services, engaging with Corporate Social Responsibility (CSR) and philanthropic institutions, enabling governance and growth, and a certified coach with Think Talent India, an HR Consulting Company.

Udupa is a Director in Agora Analytics, an HR Analytics company and serves as a member of the Advisory Board of the RV Institute of Management.

Udupa has rich corporate HR experience and conceptual knowledge in manufacturing, projects, Information Technology and the professional services industry. He started his career with Widia (India). Thereafter, he has been General Manager, HR of the Tube Investments of India, a Murugappa Group Company, Vice President-HR of Wartsila India, Head HR of Oracle India, President HR of the Adani Group and Director and Human Capital Leader for PwC India. He has done substantial original work in the areas of employee engagement, talent management, succession planning and leadership development, mergers and acquisition and culture building.

He was the HR Panel Head at Confederation of Indian Industries (CII). He has been a guest faculty at management institutions, addressed seminars, conducted workshops and programmes at the national level on quality, HR, leadership and management. He has written a few papers in academic journals, contributed a couple of chapters for a book on performance management and a case study in a book on coaching.

After graduating from St. Xavier's College, Mumbai, Udupa did a postgraduate master's programme in Personnel Management & Industrial Relations, from TATA Institute of Social Sciences, Mumbai.

He can be contacted at shrihari.udupa@gmail.com

Raghavan Mukund

Mukund is restless, experimenting with something new every couple of years. The one constant factor in the last 20 years has been training, skilling and transforming people to help them find meaning in their jobs.

Mukund is the Founder Director of Sabre Skilling Private Limited and has been involved in conducting various management, sales and customer service interventions. Sabre Skilling has trained more than 60000 people in India, China, Japan, Europe, South East Asia, Australia and the Middle East. The company has worked with 85+ brands including Titan, Samsonite, Jockey, Shell, Honeywell and Saint Gobain.

Before he turned entrepreneur, he worked in sales, marketing, product management and business management functions in multinational companies like Widia (India) and Saint Gobain for 18 years.

Mukund has also been the CEO of INDSPHINX Precision Limited, a manufacturer of precision tools for aerospace, medical, electronics and specialised machining applications. As a company head, he mentored a team of over 300 professionals in all functions. He continues to be an active director on its board.

An avid photographer and wildlife enthusiast, he usually holidays in places where there are more animals and fewer human beings.

This is his second book. His first book was *DON'T SELL. Make them BUY.*

He can be contacted at mukund@sabre-skilling.com

CHAPTER 1

The New Nomads:
Relentlessly Restless

Rajesh was a gold medallist from Indian Institute of Technology, Mumbai. He was one of the students that teachers loved. No one was surprised when he qualified and got into one of the best management institutes in the country—Indian Institute of Management, Ahmedabad. Here, again, he excelled. He came out with flying colours and was one of the first from his college to get his first job with the second highest salary ever offered to a fresher. Rajesh was very happy.

A year later, Rajesh was at his second job. The first one had been a disaster. He could not fit into the organisation. People behaved like zombies. They did what they were constantly instructed to do. Rajesh had tried his best to fit in but found that nobody had the time for him—to listen to his suggestions or his problems.

Finally, it was his classmate and friend Sanjay who offered him a way out. "Forget the large financial services sector," he said. "You don't belong there. Come and join our startup instead. You will be heard here."

Rajesh lasted at the startup for just about six months. He found that while people worked together, they had no clue what they were doing or where the company was headed. Though funds were not a problem, the company had no clear direction.

The organisation had many young people like himself, forming a well-knit group, who seemed happy to have breakfast, lunch and dinner in the office together. After six months though, Rajesh was sure the company would head nowhere. His friend Sanjay had left three months earlier to do a short-term programme in Harvard, USA. He told Rajesh before leaving that he had always wanted to pursue academics and pure sciences.

Rajesh and Sanjay are not the only early jobbers switching jobs. Why are organisations not able to hold on to people like them? Are workplaces not right incubation places for them? Were Rajesh and Sanjay unclear about what they wanted? Were their expectations not something that their workplaces could meet? Maybe so. If so, is that the problem today? That people have unrealistic expectations?

People today—restless, chasing chimera. Restlessness among people means frequent job changes and greater organisational instability.

In general, people today are restless. They are well-educated, from the best colleges and schools in the world, and are in search of that ideal place to work where they can apply their knowledge. They also want to get ahead very quickly and easily get demotivated when it does not happen. That is when they change jobs.

However, they soon realise that switching jobs, getting better pay and benefits cannot cure them of their restlessness. Very soon, they reach a stage when they do not know what they are chasing.

Freshers and youngsters are not the only ones. People in very senior positions, in the prime of their careers, suddenly leave their jobs and salaries to pursue something very unexpected—join ashrams, grow capsicum, start a school and so on. Many throw away jobs that had earned them millions and join NGOs (charitable and service organisations) to help others sustain a livelihood. These people are not old enough to retire, and a lot of them are at the peak of their careers. Clearly, a good job and compensation package are not enough to keep them satisfied. They are looking for something else.

Organisations lack stability due to people churn

Every employer today has the same complaint—most people in the organisation are constantly on the lookout for better opportunities. They are constantly seeking something "better" and something different.

At the beginning of their careers, people look for a job and financial safety. Organisations try to woo them by providing swanky offices, cafeterias, recreation facilities, social events and, of course, attractive pay packages.

After a while, though, this fails to satisfy. They begin to look around, change jobs, and, sometimes, even careers, all in the hope of finding "meaning".

From the organisation's point of view, this constant seeking something "more", and the resultant churn in the workplace is a major stumbling block and comes in the way of meeting growth targets. Ultimately, it is the right people with the right skills that help companies grow their top and bottom lines—figures that are all-important to the investors, shareholders, collaborators, group company ideologies and the board.

To get around the problem, organisations resort to lateral recruitment and higher compensation packages.

Lateral hires come with their own set of problems. While they have the necessary domain knowledge and experience, they do not always fit into the organisational culture and role. New entrants mean new teams. Managers have to deal with the additional challenge of trying to make new entrants part of a team instead of focusing on the job at hand—a challenge that can lead to more dissatisfaction.

The new recruit often comes with baggage from the previous company, and if the feeling of "I am used to doing things differently" kicks in, there is the danger of the person not being able to fit in, not being able to work efficiently, and in extreme cases, just leaving.

If the newly recruited manager tries to impose a different culture on the team, it only creates confusion. If things don't work out, the new person either leaves or creates a situation where the other members of the team leave.

Consequently, organisations today lack stability—a situation born out of conflicting expectations. While organisations are looking at what makes business sense for them, people are looking for quick personal gains and benefits.

The chart below represents this graphically—the dichotomy between the self-interest of the organisation and its people.

Dichotomy – Self interest

ORGANISATION

PEOPLE

Profit Maximization
Share holder value
Brand
Market position
Valuation
Aggressive grpwth
Quick results
Engaged people

Purse maximisation
Fast growth
Instant gratification
Personal growth
Self identity
Status

> HR attempts are not very successful... no stickiness of employees... constant churn in the organisation... expectation dichotomy.
>
> Great cafeterias and gyms do not seem to make people happy. People continue to leave. There is an expectation dichotomy between the organisation and its people.

HR heads are leaving no stone unturned to stem this flow. They try more employee engagement activities, cross-functional interactions, training and team-building workshops. But company events, a great cafeteria and gym, and the latest electronic gadgets do not seem to make people happy. People continue to leave.

Organisations' offer of carrots fails to bridge the divide or meet people's expectations. This is graphically shown below. Organisations inputs are centred on providing more and more salaries, incentives and facilities, whereas employees are actually trying to find meaning and fulfilment once their basic necessities are met.

There is a huge expectation mismatch, as is explained below.

Dichotomy – Offerings & Expectation

Adding to the restlessness and discontent in the workplace is the huge disparity in the compensation offered to the CEO and the others. In recent times, this disparity has become so accentuated that the CEO package is a few hundred times more than the median salary.

While becoming high-salaried people in senior positions may seem like an attractive goal to work towards, in reality, only a very small percentage of people actually make the cut to get there. This, once again, leads to restlessness among the majority who prefer to seek greener pastures elsewhere.

High CEO packages have another adverse outcome. In the race to protect his/her own bonus and incentive, the CEO ends up curtailing investments in people, stunting their growth, which is a vital requirement for organisation building.

> **Success craving—possible reason for the divide and people's restlessness**

Global management approaches, greatly influenced by western thought, have leant heavily on what we call the "hard" side of the business. Aggressive leadership, relentless business focus, strategies and technology have been touted as being all-important for businesses to thrive and prosper. While these, without doubt, are necessary means to grow the business, too single-minded a focus leads to eventual neglect of the "soft" side—the people.

Even organisations that claim that people are "critical" to their business rarely see them as anything but a "resource". While they advocate recruiting people with the right skills, regularly evaluating performance, providing training opportunities and incentives—all of it is done with an eye to improve business performance. At the slightest hint of a downturn in business, the "downsizing" exercise starts. People are discarded like unwanted objects to cut down costs and shore up the bottom line.

At the same time, the organisation irrationally expects the people to "engage" themselves diligently to the tasks assigned to them and perform with passion to grow the top and bottom line. A good pay package, facilities at work to make the workplace physically comfortable and providing them with training inputs to "develop" them professionally is considered a fair quid pro quo for the people to perform at their full potential. The interactions, as one can see, are purely transactional, and there is a distinct lack of human touch or spirit. There is a success craving on both sides, which creates a big divide. This creates a lot of restlessness in people.

I pay, you perform does not address the "soft side of business".

If people say "THANK GOD IT IS FRIDAY" with immense relief, then something is not right.

Organisations constantly push people to improve processes to maximise business returns. They use business goals achieved as indicators to evaluate and control people's performance by rewarding good performance with pay rises, promotion and bonuses.

They conduct periodic surveys to capture employee satisfaction and employee engagement. At the slightest hint of dissatisfaction, organisations jump up to hand out everything from freebies and birthday greetings to flexi-time and work-from-home options.

But at the end of the day (or rather, the week), if people still wait to say in relief, "Thank God, it is Friday"—then that is reasonable proof that the work has neither been satisfying or meaningful.

Obviously, these measures fail to motivate and engage employees. Surveys by reputed organisations have shown that not even 15% of people are "engaged" and applying themselves fully to their job.

(Gallop survey results discussed in this book in Chapter 6.) March 2016, Gallup poll on employee disengagement in the US.

So, what are we missing here? Could it be the fact that human beings are not machines, and they expect to be acknowledged as such? That they look for support and understanding with empathy to do the job better?

Individuals and organisations chase different successes—both trying to make an impact.

Success and satisfaction—organisations and people want both but often fail to understand what it really entails.

Individuals aspire success—in terms of promotions, better salaries and climbing the organisational hierarchy. After a while, however, realisation sets in that this does not translate into satisfaction, contentment, peace and happiness. People's definition of "success" changes with time (dealt with in more detail in Chapter 3).

True success and satisfaction come only when they can honestly say, "I find meaning in what I do" and "I am happy doing what I do". And this sense of fulfilment comes only when they know that they are contributing to making a positive impact.

Organisations—like people—are also chasing success. But they are rarely in sync with individual success. Organisations feel they are successful by being better than their competitors and having a larger share of the market. Often, if they cannot beat competition, they buy them. In this game to create more shareholder wealth, people become secondary.

Chasing profits becomes so important that many a time, organisations take shortcuts and even compromise the customer. New initiatives for growth tend to be short-term oriented, and this kind of growth is difficult for the organisation to sustain for long. Therefore, the organisation too changes its definition of "success" with time and maturity.

Somehow, both the organisation and the employees fail to understand what the "success" they are chasing really is.

There is no alignment between the organisation's and people's goals.

The leadership usually develops and deploys a "vision" and attempts to put down what the organisation would want to achieve in the future. In most cases, this vision remains a statement of "business goals", talking mainly about growing top and bottom line, increasing market share, and satisfying customers and shareholders. It is often seen as a tool to create an alignment between people and the organisation goals.

But when organisations' visions are purely business oriented, they are unable to attract the buy-in from everyone and, therefore, unable to get a commitment from people on a sustained basis.

Some companies have found the bridge for the divide.

Some companies, though—like the TATA Group—seem to have found the right balance. What makes these companies stand out?

TATA Steel, for example, took a unique approach to business. The group was founded on a philosophy to cater to the purpose of "doing good to society" and "creating wealth for a nation".

TCS—another TATA Group Company—is not even the best paymaster in the IT industry. It is a very large organisation with over 400,000 employees, where the path to the top is long and arduous. But, despite that, it has the lowest attrition rate in the industry. What makes people stay on there? Could it be the culture that places emphasis on strong human values and encourages people to look for something beyond the run of the mill business numbers?

In short:

- Sops that organisations dole out do not guarantee commitment and loyalty.

- Selfish interests dominate both people and organisations— they are both chasing materialistic success without being sensitive to each other.

In rare cases, when organisations bridge this dichotomy and create synergy, they create magic. People are filled with an enthusiasm to achieve and enrich themselves in a way that is not necessarily materialistic. They begin to see meaning in what they do.

Organisations that have found this magic are able to provide people a meaningful engagement to contribute with passion and alignment to the vision and the goals.

When individuals contribute to a purpose*, beyond their own professional success, they find true meaning in life.

In an organisation that provides a purposeful engagement and environment, people find congruence of their own purpose of finding meaning in their work and align it with the company purpose. The moment the alignment of purpose is achieved, there is a release of positive energy. Commitment to the organisation follows, restlessness disappears, and employees begin to take ownership of delivering the purpose.

MAGIC

Synergy through
congruence of
Organisation
PURPOSE

And MEANING
to people

Enabled by process

Treated as a
Resource (Not as a
human being)

Limited by
Dichotomies

CHAPTER 2

The Widia Story: Purposeful Leadership Anchored in Values

....

"Purpose drives behaviour. Purpose affirms trust. Trust affirms purpose, and together, they forge individuals into a working team. The CEO exemplifies the purpose by living it and building programmes derived from it."

US Army General McChrystal—in his book *Team of Teams*

I met Lakshmi at one of my workshops. A regional accountant in a private bank, she was good at her job, a sincere worker and put in long hours. But for some reason, her boss, Kumar, had taken a dislike to her. He constantly picked on her and found fault with her.

Some of the others in the office had found ways of 'managing' the boss, but Lakshmi was too straightforward a person to play politics.

One morning, the strained relations between Kumar and Lakshmi hit a new low. He was furious with her because the monthly reports had not been sent on time. She told him that she had been waiting for him to approve some of the bills for reimbursement from regional managers. They claimed to have been incurred for "client development", but it did not look right to her.

"Just pass them," Kumar had thundered. "The RMs may have bent rules to satisfy customers, but so what?"

"I will handle it if there is a query. That's none of your business," he said angrily when she protested.

It seemed like the last straw. Instead of being appreciated for her diligence, she was being reprimanded. She had grown up with strong beliefs and a value system that seemed to be out of place here. She was perplexed by the ethics, where the boss' intent was just to keep the head office off his back. The only rule in place seemed to be "Do whatever you want as long as you don't get caught".

"I always wanted to complete my Chartered Accountancy Certifications and work with a large company," she told me. "Now I have started to wonder, is corporate life like this everywhere? Am I being foolish to expect anything better?"

**– Mukund R, one of the three authors,
a former Widian and now a corporate trainer**

Lakshmi's story set us thinking about the difference between her experience and that of Widians. 'What set Widia apart?' was a long drawn out discussion and one that we have attempted to answer. To fully explain our stance, we have to go back a very long way, to the beginning of Widia India itself.

In the late 1960s, Krupp Widia of Germany set up operations in India to make tungsten carbide cutting tools for the emerging Indian manufacturing sector catering to the major public sector and mining companies. The idea was that locally manufactured tools would be cheaper and more easily accessible to these organisations.

One of the first people to set up Widia India was R. Srinivasan (RS) (also a co-author), who was till then working for Widia in Germany. He was sent down to head the plant in India, together with a German (Dr. H. Roettger) who became the first managing director.

With little inputs from the German parent, the two had to rely on their own motivation to drive the company forward. The German MD soon returned to his home country, and R. Srinivasan quickly formed a key leadership team and gave it the mandate to lead the organisation to success.

The new arm had to start from scratch. Other than a moderate technology transfer, it had practically no other assistance from Widia Germany.

The initial years were difficult. But even in those trying years, where the leadership team had to steer the company through a number of challenges, one thing was sacrosanct. The company was rooted in its belief in basic human values like honesty, integrity, respect and care for others, and transparency in all its dealings with employees or the external world, including customers and the government officials.

NO COMPROMISES – Widia stuck to its principles

The emphasis on doing the things the right way often resulted in more struggle, delays and loss of time, but the company steadfastly stuck to its principles.

At that time, Widia did not have formally written down value statements, but it soon became an unwritten rule that ethics would never be compromised and the company would take up all challenges that came its way without resorting to shortcuts.

Until the early 90s, it was still the "licence permit raj" era in India. Practically every business activity needed permission and approval from designated authorities. Imports were subjected to special import licensing rules. Not a single screw could be imported without an import licence from the DGTD (Director General of Technical Development) sitting in Delhi.

Given Widia's strict ethical standards, this meant that the company's leadership ended up making multiple four-hour flights to Delhi just to meet and get permission from the *babus* (officials) sitting there. There was no question of adopting the easier, if less correct, path of paying speed money. Many times, the emphasis on doing things the right way resulted in more struggle, protracted delays, and loss of time and opportunities, but the company steadfastly stuck to its principles.

Widia had a clear though unstated purpose.

Widia was not just supplying the right tools. It was committed to helping customers improve their productivity.

Back in the 60s and 70s, India had just started its industrialisation journey. The goal at Widia was to build an organisation that stood out—a safe and challenging environment for people to work in and contribute towards improving the performance of its customers. The company firmly believed that it had a purpose, and that was to help its customers (the Indian manufacturing industry) **improve their productivity and performance and to improve the standard of living of its people.**

Widia was not content with just supplying the right tools. Other competitors were already doing that. It was committed to helping customers with technical inputs to use the tools in an optimal manner and get better output. Improving customer productivity became the purpose of its existence. There was an unspoken pride among the people, and they were firm in their belief that they were making a difference to the country's emerging manufacturing landscape.

Interestingly, this came at a time when management lexicon worldwide had yet to make any mention of the concept of "purpose" for businesses.

 Larger purpose over profit Widia chose to keep the commercial aspects aside and reached for bigger things.

Being a late entrant in the field, Widia found that many major customers in the business had already tied up with suppliers—Widia's key competitors. Hindustan Machine Tools (Hindustan Machine Tools), then the largest machine tool manufacturer in India, was one such customer that Widia approached. The Chairman of Hindustan Machine Tools sent the Widia team back saying that he was quite happy with the standard tools being supplied by vendors like Sandvik. Sandvik, then the world leader in their field, had a plant in Pune and had well entrenched itself with Hindustan Machine Tools as a supplier.

Despite the first rejection, Widia kept trying. Finally, the Chairman of Hindustan Machine Tools Dr. S.M. Patil, a doyen of Machine Tool Industry, gave in. There was still no opening in the main factory, he said, but if Widia wanted some business, they could look at supplying tools for the Hindustan Machine Tools watch factory. Hindustan Machine Tools was just then diversifying into watches, and these tools were then being imported. The import duties were very high in those days, and Hindustan Machine Tools wanted to substitute imports.

This was a major breakthrough and a cause to celebrate. But it was also a challenge to worry about. Watch-making tools were quite complex and were completely outside the scope of Widia's manufacturing capabilities. In addition to the manufacturing complexity, the commercial proposition of making these tools was not attractive. It was little wonder then that the other local competitors had stayed away from manufacturing these tools, and Hindustan Machine Tools had to continue to import the tools at very high costs.

The Widia team decided to jump at the opportunity and keep aside the commercial aspect. To produce these tools was a big challenge and involved a lot of hard work, investment of time and resources, but the success was a reward in itself. When Widia was finally able to make and supply these tools, they won the deep appreciation of the Hindustan Machine Tools senior management.

The project success also opened other doors. Widia also started to supply the standard range of tools to HMT's main business—the machine tool factory. The company had found a long-term way to start increasing revenues despite the initial indifference from their customer.

The company viewed customer orders not merely from the margin/profit angle but focused on meeting the need behind the need of the customer in a true sense of partnership. Widia had gone ahead with its sense of purpose to improve productivity and had taken it upon itself to solve customer problems. Though this was not the best decision in the commercial sense, it had helped to pave the way for sustainable growth in business. With this kind of approach, Widia soon earned itself the reputation among customers as a reliable and serious partner who they could depend on.

> **Widians believed Indians were second to none.**

Widians also had deep-seated confidence and belief that Indians were second to none and could do as well as, if not better than, their German collaborators.

It was the 1970s, just around that time, India's war with Pakistan for the liberation and formation of Bangladesh was on. The Indian army needed an indigenous source of vital amour piercing shots for their anti-tank ammunition. The core consisted of a heavy solid tungsten carbide penetrator with special tungsten nickel alloy nose. The Department of Defence Production approached Widia India to manufacture these cores and noses.

Once again, this was an area where Widia had no knowledge or experience. The process was totally different from Widia's core business of manufacturing cutting tools. Moreover, the German principal did not want to have anything to do with the production of armaments.

But the country's needs were great, and an order was placed. Under the Defence of India rules, the government had the power to take over the entire facility to take up manufacture of these items if it so decided. There really was no option for Widia but to agree to try and make them. But the leadership team also recognised that this was necessary in the national interest and applied themselves very seriously to the task. The government was willing to pay advance money for this effort, and the infusion of funds at this point turned out to be a timely blessing and bailed Widia out of cash flow problems.

The defence order and the opening of opportunities with large corporates set Widia on a path of growth. Widia's decision to put national interest above all other company policies and priorities helped to lay the foundation for building a great organisation. Widia was able to make decisions without contradictions as the leadership addressed the **purpose**.

> **The purpose and value system percolated from leaders to everybody in the organisation.**

The leadership's conduct ensured that purpose and values permeated into the teams until it became part of who they were.

The leaders' single-minded focus on the **purpose** rubbed off on the rest of the organisation—not to give in to an easier route when faced with a difficulty became a standard practice within the company.

Slowly but surely, Widians started thinking differently, following the example set by the leadership. Together with the **purpose**, basic human values were also instilled into the people. An unwritten value system flowed from the leadership's conduct and evolved organically within the organisation. The leadership's conduct ensured that **purpose** and values permeated into the teams until it became part of who they were. Consistency in the leader's thought, words and actions only strengthened the **purpose** and the value system.

The emphasis on basic human values became apparent as early as the pre-employment interviews. Job seekers were quizzed on more than just their professional abilities. They were also evaluated on the values they considered important. The aim was to recruit people who understood their duties so that they could eventually become responsible members of the Widia team. The recruitment team assessed candidates (most of them around 20 years old) on their willingness to take responsibility for more than just their personal needs and wellbeing. For example, they were asked about what they would do for the family back in the village and siblings still at school. Widia believed the candidate's personal belief system was a critical indicator of his/her ability and willingness to take greater responsibility and ownership in his/her career too.

The importance of taking responsibility and doing their best to find solutions was once again drilled into early jobbers when they became part of the Widia team. The expectation was that every employee would cross the boundary of self-interest and work for something beyond that.

This policy of recruiting people ingrained with a sense of basic human values and willing to take on responsibility beyond selfish considerations won the hearts and minds of the employees. In turn, they gave their very best to Widia. The Widia leadership provided them guidance not only related to their work but also in their personal lives, to help them develop into capable and responsible human beings. The organisation trained them to succeed both in their jobs and their lives.

Sunil Taneja was a freshly recruited graduate engineer who had joined Widia in the late 70s. As part of his induction process, he was required to work on the machines. He hated this, as he thought it was an operator's job. After all, he was an engineer.

One day, when he was still in his training period, the managing director found him standing on the shop floor with his hands in his pockets, watching the operator do his job. He thought he could learn things merely by watching other people do the work.

The managing director called him to his room. "Do you have any purpose in life?" he asked him. "Are you planning to learn anything by working with your own hands, or are you planning to waste time idling and watching others work?"

Something pricked Taneja that day. The fact that the managing director had called a mere trainee engineer to his room to ask him fundamental questions set him thinking. "That was the turning point of my life," says Taneja. "I discovered that everybody should have a purpose and should work towards fulfilling that purpose."

Today, Taneja is a successful entrepreneur, employing 400 people and manufacturing precision tools and exporting them to over 30 advanced countries like Germany and Japan. He attributes his evolution into a responsible businessperson to that little incident decades ago.

> **" Mistakes were forgiven. Dishonesty was not.**

As the basic human value system was ingrained, the expectation from the employees regarding honesty and integrity was very high—they were constantly encouraged to faithfully report all work-related issues and problems, lapses that occurred and mistakes that were made. There was limited supervision around to monitor people, even in night shifts. Even critical processes continued round the clock without supervision.

A related concern also was how to deal with lapses, failures and mistakes that people made unsupervised. The leadership realised that if mistakes were dealt with severely, people would stop reporting them or shift blame or disown the problem. The management made a decision that failures could be accepted, with the implicit expectation that they would not be repeated. The need was to create a sense of "responsibility and ownership".

Widia's message to its people remained unwaveringly the same.

"Think of the company as your own. Remember that if you do well, the company prospers. If the company fails, your own future is at stake."

This atmosphere, free of fear of reprimand or consequences, allowed not just the leaders at various levels but everyone in the company to speak their minds, share their ideas, point out what was wrong or needed change and propelled the organisation forward.

Occasionally, however, there were lapses of integrity, and dealing with them became a challenge for the leaders.

There was the incident of a security-guard-cum-mail-clerk who made a reimbursement claim for an amount that was more than the actual. When this was discovered, the leaders were in a dilemma on how to deal with this. On one side, the organisation was emphasising honesty and ethics. On the other, there was pressure on the leaders to forgive the man as the amount was "just a small" one. They were sure this would not be repeated after the person was counselled. But the final decision was made to dismiss him from service even for that small misappropriation.

Though the amount involved wasn't much, the message that needed to go out was that no transgression would be tolerated. The decision reiterated the emphasis placed on a value system and behaviour and doing what was good for the company in the long term—all beliefs that had become core to Widia. Genuine mistakes could be overlooked, but there was zero tolerance for deliberate lapses in integrity.

On values—the organisation stuck to its stance.

In the early 70s, the Government of India extended the excise duty to all tools, and Widia's products fell under this. All manufactured goods could be dispatched from the factory only after duty had been paid. An excise department inspector was posted on-site to ensure compliance. At that time, a common practice among companies was to pay the official a regular *hafta*—a bribe to clear the goods. The inspector posted to Widia expected the same thing and sent feelers to the manager in charge. Widia, of course, refused to budge from its position. No bribes would be paid.

The consequences of this decision were that there were more delays and unreasonable penalties, followed by tiresome legal procedures to appeal against the unjust penalties. But Widia stuck it out, and soon enough, the higher-ups in the excise department realised that the company was steadfast in upholding its principles. In fact, the company found out later that the department had begun to use Widia as a "punishment posting" for its errant officers, knowing fully well that no inspector could make any extra cash there!

The leadership was anchored in values even during testing times, created a spirit of doing the right things and stopped people from doing the wrong things, although that would have been easier and faster.

Respect and care for people builds trust.

A fundamental foundation for the creation of an outstanding organisation is recognition of basic human values.

While integrity and ethics were important, Widia placed equal importance on basic human values like respect and care. This included acknowledging and respecting all people as individuals in their own right and listening to their problems. In fact, one of the fundamental foundations for the creation of an outstanding organisation, according to Widia, is recognition of basic human values.

Studies and surveys have observed that the biggest reason for an employee leaving an organisation is rarely the salary. Most exits come from a feeling of not being important to the organisation, not being respected and cared for. This feeling also arises when there is a lack of involvement from the bosses or the job is not challenging enough or there is a lack of integrity in business.

At Widia, this was hardly ever an issue. The leadership held in high regard the values of contribution, integrity, care, concern, fairness, equity and belief in people. People were challenged to do better and more complex things. No one was asked to do anything against their conscience. No one was expected to "please the bosses". On the contrary, people were expected to raise their voice against wrongdoings by anyone. There were no henchmen; there were no favourites. Meritocracy ruled.

 Free access to leadership and freedom to disagree.

People at Widia had unrestricted access to the leadership, who always found the time to listen patiently to the employee's problems or ideas. This created a fearless environment where people could share their ideas, however outlandish. They were confident of getting some resonance from the leaders, either in the form of useful suggestions or a go-ahead to experiment without any fear of failure or reprimand. This enabled people to develop into "intrapreneurs". The result—Widia has produced a disproportionately large number of successful CEOs and entrepreneurs who are making waves in their domains.

In the early 80s, India went through a period of very high trade union activism. Widia also saw some strikes, which were formally 'resolved' by the labour commissioner but led to increased tension on the shop floor. Not surprisingly, it began to impact both productivity and relationships at the workplace.

During this phase, the union wanted to put up an anti-management communication on the notice board in the canteen. As a head of HR handling union relations, I felt that the content of the notice was provocative and refused permission. Annoyed, the union wanted to escalate the matter to R. Srinivasan, the managing director, who was the ultimate authority.

In the meantime, I explained the matter to R. Srinivasan.

He absorbed all that I said. Then he said, "If I were in your place, I would have given permission to put up the notice."

Hurt by this apparent lack of support for my decision, I retorted in anger, "You are only saying this because you need to answer the German authorities about the frequent disruptions at work."

Trying to calm me down, he pointed out the consequences of withholding permission. "It might lead to another strike, the labour department will have to get involved once again, and the department officials will begin to question the maturity of the Widia leadership."

In short, he did not think it was worth fighting about.

"It is just a notice, even if it is anti-management and is strongly worded. It would be unwise to let something minor like this precipitate into a strike," he reasoned.

I was still not convinced and continued to argue. Finally, R. Srinivasan told me to take a call on it and assured me of his support, whatever my decision may be.

I grudgingly told him I would permit the notice to be displayed.

In any other organisation, I would have been sacked then and there for insubordination! Looking back at that incident, I realise that in the Widia environment, it was never a question of who was more powerful but what was right for the organisation.

There were the usual disagreements about performance ratings, increments, promotions, but deep down, everyone knew that the organisation encouraged growth and worked for the larger good.

There was never a contradiction between what was said and what was followed. Trust and faith in the leadership were never in question.

– Shrihari Udupa, co-author of the book

Animal leadership is simple and uncontested. Human leadership is complex.

Humans don't follow blindly. They choose—to either follow or not.

Unlike in the animal world, where leadership is very simple and uncontested, human leader-follower dynamics are complex.

The elephant matriarch leads her herd, as she is the most experienced and knows how to keep the herd safe and lead them to food and water. In Kenya and Tanzania, just one wildebeest leads a million others across the African landscape, as they famously run together in search of food, water and survival because the followers trust their leader blindly.

Humans don't follow blindly. They choose—to either follow or not.

When there is a strong buy-in to the leaders' ideas and philosophy, leaders and followers are in sync, and all transactions are smooth. The buy-in happens when leaders foster an environment that enables people evolution based on attitude, aptitude and potential. This generates a workforce that puts in its best and is self-driven and motivated.

On the other hand, when there is no buy-in, people are not aligned to leaders and their way of thinking. Just getting them to perform tasks becomes a task in itself.

It creates a workplace that is highly supervised, where people have to be constantly instructed, monitored and pushed. People do not feel empowered. They hesitate to take decisions even with regard to the smallest of issues and turn to their bosses for direction.

This state of 'helplessness' leads to a slow and continuous erosion of motivation. All creativity and innovation get killed. Merely carrying out the boss' directions, certainly, is not a satisfying state for the individual. If the people's work satisfaction depends on leaders, leaders too are dependent on their followers for the fulfilment of individual goals.

Leader's personal conduct builds trust...

If the leader has to inspire his/her team, his/her personal conduct and behaviour has a huge impact.

People buy in to a leader who shows congruence in thought, words and actions. Leaders who say what they think, are frank and open and do what they say reflect a behaviour that is predictable, and this helps to create an atmosphere of trust. If the leader has to inspire his/her team to contribute its best for the development of the organisation, his/her personal conduct and behaviour has the maximum impact.

It always comes as a shock and a let-down when leaders of large organisations, once hailed as visionaries, come crashing down from their pedestals. Unfortunately, a large number of them, in recent times, have been caught breaking some basic rules for personal benefit.

Carlos Goshn, Chairman Nissan (Under-reporting personal income)

J. Y. Lee, Executive Vice Chairman, Samsung (Bribery, Embezzlement)

Martin Winterkorn, CEO Volkswagen (Illegal software to beat emission norms)

Chanda Kochar, CEO, ICICI Bank (Conflict of Interest in doling out loans)

Brian Crutcher, CEO, Texas Instrument (Violating Code of Conduct)

Binny Bansal, Flipkart Cofounder (Affair with employee)

Roger Ailes, CEO, Fox News (Sexual harassment)

– Source: *Economic Times* 25th Nov., 2018-11-26

Understanding values and binding people with purpose and *holistic* values...

Most companies have a set of business ethics in place. Many of them articulate and put up their **core values**. However, at Widia, leaders believed that business ethics alone was not enough to bind people and empower them to work without contradictions.

So the Widia leadership included the equally important concepts of **basic human values*** and **dharmic values*** to be practised and ingrained in people. For instance, they believed that the way a person is treated (human values) has a huge impact on his/her engagement and contribution to the growth and progress of an organisation.

The values are classified into three parts for ease of understanding:

Basic Human Values—these are values we learn from our families, school, institutions and friends such as:

- Honesty

- Integrity

- Respect

- Care

While parents, teachers and childhood stories stress the importance of values in our personal lives, no one tells us that it is no different at the workplace. The values that we share become the basis for trust between people. And trust is everything for a binding relationship.

Dharmic values are nothing but a code of conduct regulating a person's work and activities.

Another set of human values of a slightly higher order are the ones that this book will refer to as **dharmic values**. These come with maturity (both of the individual and the organisation).

Examples of **dharmic values** are:

- Selflessness

- Spirit of service

- Compassion

- Empathy

In a business environment, basic human values are important for all interactions and help to build efficient teams. Dharmic values are generally associated with individuals in their personal lives. They are nothing but a code of conduct regulating a person's work and activities to follow a righteous path.

The quintessence of dharma is that one should not do to others what would be disliked by oneself.

Some people may argue that **righteousness** has no place in business. But when organisations are expected to be "good corporate citizens", a rethink is warranted on this subject.

Leaders can steer dharmic values steep through the organisation through their conduct. It then becomes the culture, which guides the conduct of people in various situations and enables them to make principled choices.

From its early days, Widia had been following these principles as a matter of course. It was this approach that was responsible for unleashing the hidden potential in individuals, which drove them from strength to strength. Widia pioneered various changes in the 80s and 90s such as quality movement, TQM, Business Process Re-engineering and business excellence in the Indian corporate world. Widia was the second company in the country to embrace the ISO as early as 1991.

Over a period of time, when the company became reasonably stable, the business goals subtly changed. Widia now wanted to scale up and climb higher in the pecking order. Size, market share and dominance became important.

In the next few years, Widia achieved some of these goals and reached a satisfactory degree of performance. At this point, however, a sense of déjà vu began to set in. With the major struggles behind them, work somehow became less fulfilling. The sense of purpose that drove Widia in the earlier years seemed to have become less sharp. Business goals and rapid growth became the focus, and although the values were not compromised, the sense of purpose, which was the aligning and binding force, took a back seat.

While the day-to-day struggles continued as usual, the leadership began to be bothered about **more fundamental** questions. In spite of all the achievements in the marketplace, the leaders continued to be restless. There were niggling doubts. Was annual budgeting, chasing numbers and developing customers an end in itself? What was the organisation trying to achieve? Everything suddenly seemed uncertain and hazy. **New questions arose—questions of identity and purpose of existence**.

It took quite some churning and external help to realise that organisations also needed to go beyond numbers and profits. Across the organisation, people seemed to be feeling empty and were looking for some fulfilment.

These questions were constantly bothering the leadership, which then threw them open to internal stakeholders.

The extended and in-depth discussions that followed took the team back to the very beginning when they started out with the commitment to make a difference and "improve productivity" of the customer and the country. The success of the 80s seemed to have clouded the **purpose**, which had driven the company to what it was. The purpose was lost in the euphoria of success and market leadership. However, this **success*** did not satisfy the people.

At the end of the discussions, everyone agreed that the topmost need was to write down the **Purpose and Operating Values** that resonated with everyone so that they could work together as partners rather than rivals. Finally, Widia put together a **purpose statement**—not one handed down by the leadership but one that was arrived at jointly by the leaders and the employees.

The purpose statement formed the core of a pocket booklet shown below.

Purpose

Our purpose is:

To enhance the productivity of industries by being the leader in supplying high technology, quality engineering products and services,

– by being responsive to the needs of customers, employees, business associates, shareholders, the community and society at large,

– through an organisation of committed, highly skilled, motivated and satisfied people striving for innovation and excellence,

and

achieve continual growth in sales and profits through fair means in all dealings.

Along with the purpose, the operating values were also written down.

Holistic VALUES = Basic human + Dharmic + Business Ethics

Basic "Human" Values
Honesty
Integrity
Respect
Care

"Dharmic" Values
Selflessness
Spirit of service
Compassion
Empathy

Business Ethics
Probity and ethics
Conformance to laws
Governance and disclosure
Fairness & Equity

In this book, we are defining this as _Holistic_ Values. These are an amalgam of basic human values, dharmic values and business ethics.

This documentation of what had been happening in the company almost since inception helped it realign itself and work with renewed vigour and enthusiasm.

At the beginning of every meeting, it became a custom for one person to read this set of operating values aloud. This would be followed by discussions of real work life developments in the context of the values. The book itself became a binding force, and all new entrants were able to imbibe the principles quickly. The operating values helped department heads and team leaders to make the right choices and decisions when faced with conflicts.

Interestingly, one of the most respected organisations in India today, the TATA Group has a very simple and similarly articulated guiding principles called the TCOC—The TATA Code of Conduct.

The more commonly used **business ethics** tend to be compliance-directed, aimed at ensuring that there is no hanky-panky or violation of the law and that the organisation complies with business rules and regulations, does not cheat or bribe, discloses correct data and information and does not accept wrongdoing.

Operating values, Widia believed, combined business ethics with basic human values and helped to bind people together, empower them and help them make decisions free of fear. It was aimed at promoting a healthy work environment.

Encouraged by the process of creating a physical booklet of the **Purpose and Operating Values**, the leadership decided to repeat the exercise with the representatives of the trade union. Equal numbers of members of the leadership and internal trade union representatives participated in a workshop facilitated to address the questions troubling the minds of the people.

It was during this retreat that there was a surprising revelation. Discussions led to the discovery that all internal stakeholders—including the employees and union representatives, who were at various levels in their own personal evolution—had very similar aspirations of growth. They all felt the need to contribute, make a larger difference to society, impact lives and leave a legacy.

The **Purpose and Operating Values** document gained further strength from the discussions to become the most important booklet, guiding all matters within the company.

Widia declared these values publicly as the ones that the leadership lived by. This document gave the direction, enabled decision-making and ensured consistency and uniformity of approach/behaviour. The clarity that this provided made the working more harmonious, created a flow of positivity and brought about a higher level of engagement among all stakeholders.

Holistic Values enunciation and alignment to purpose results in lesser conflicts and better outcomes.

Holistic VALUES = Basic human + Dharmic + Business Ethics

Basic "Human" Values	"Dharmic" Values	Business Ethics
Honesty	Selflessness	Probity and ethics
Integrity	Spirit of service	Conformance to laws
Respect	Compassion	Governance and disclosure
Care	Empathy	Fairness & Equity

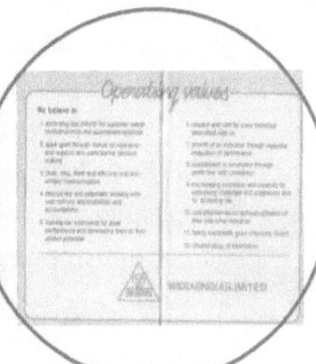

Operating values

We believe in:

1. according top *priority* for *customer needs* through prompt and appropriate response.

2. *team spirit* through mutual co-operation and support and participative decision making.

3. clear, crisp, *frank* and effective oral and written communication.

4. desciplined and *systematic working* with well defined responsibilities and accountability.

5. *training* our employees for *peak performance* and developing them to their utmost potential.

6. *respect and care* for every individual associated with us.

7. growth of an individual through *objective evaluation* of performance.

8. commitment to excellence through perfection and *consistency.*

9. encouraging innovation and creativity by *welcoming challenges* and suggestions and by *accepting risk.*

10. cost effectiveness by optimum utilisation of time and other resources.

11. being responsible good corporate citizen.

12. dissemination of information.

WIDIA(INDIA)LIMITED

The Widia **purpose** became part of the collective consciousness. People were able to connect their work directly or indirectly to the task of improving industrial productivity and outcomes for their customers. At once, this provided meaning to the jobs. When a problem was solved at the customer's end, it gave the people a sense of satisfaction and fulfilment to know that their work had improved the customer's experience and that, in some small way, they had made some difference. With each success, the people got more and more engaged with what they were doing, and the organisation's success became their success as well.

It led to the opening up of newer channels for growth and even impacted diversification and business strategies. Coming up with new solutions was not only good for business, but it also gave the team a sense of fulfilment in **making a difference**.

One of the best stories around the high level of engagement is the one that eventually led to the formation of a completely new division—the Widia SPM (Special Purpose Machine) division.

In the mid-70s, the top management at Telco, the present TATA Motors, approached Widia for the manufacture of a special "gun drill"—a crankshaft oil-hole drill, which could drill small-diameter long holes—to be used in its truck manufacturing plant in Pune. Tata Motors did not want to rely on imported gun drills.

These were very special tools, and Widia did not have the required technology. But the team was keen on being part of Telco's big indigenisation effort.

After months of struggle and numerous failures, Widia engineers finally managed to produce tools that worked on the Special Purpose Machine in Pune.

The story does not stop here.

Application engineers at Widia felt that these tools could be of use to other Widia customers too. It offered a vastly more efficient and effective way to make the long holes, and the customers welcomed it. But there was a problem. To use the tool, customers also needed to have Special Purpose Machines, which could only be imported at that time.

So it remained just a thought until one young engineer had an audacious proposal. 'Why not make the machine itself?' he asked.

It was an idea wildly beyond Widia's expertise. But it slowly began to take root and grew stronger and stronger, and eventually, the project got the required approval of the Board of Directors, as well as a licence from the Government of India.

Widia pursued it with great energy, and after sustained effort, the Widia SPM Division "WIDMA" was born. Until today, this continues to be a very successful and profitable operation.

This was possible because of the team's complete involvement with the project and its full commitment to customer interests and requirements. Equally importantly, there was freedom for all Widians to discuss their ideas and suggestions and see them taken to their logical end. A lot of times (as in the WIDMA case), it opened up new avenues for growth for the company.

At Widia, the managing director was not the only one charting out strategies for growth. Anyone could do it!

This, we believe, was possible only because the organisation had a clearly articulated **purpose**, a set of *Holistic* Values and an open work environment where people could interact without any fear or constraints, which in turn provided people with fulfilment and meaning.

What this meant was that across the organisation, there was congruence in the thinking. The alignment of the purpose and values became so strong that all the stakeholders owned it. In any situation, people at all levels were clear about what they needed to do. All decisions were guided by the overall purpose. There was no ambiguity or any need to check with the bosses, and they felt empowered.

Even new entrants soon understood the bigger picture. Every individual could find the relevance of that purpose in his or her own role, whether it was serving the customer, enhancing productivity or enhancing internal quality, productivity and processes. The focus shifted from just compliance to creating excellence, contributing and enabling the purpose. The organisation soon became a vehicle for individuals to contribute, make a difference and live a meaningful life.

People began to own the purpose of Widia and went to any lengths to make it a reality in their own ways. Creativity, energy and commitment thrived as the employees understood the true purpose of the company.

There were no doubts regarding trust, faith in people, transparency and integrity in action or the purpose of existence. It was not money and profit alone that the organisation was chasing. It was not individual success or selfish aggrandisement that the leadership was promoting. There was a fair level of understanding that the organisation was about impacting industrial productivity and thereby, quality of life, contributing to the growth of people, society and the nation.

Employees jumped in, added to the energy and kept up a strong flow for forty years. The leadership in Widia had enabled this in people.

A leader should certainly be purposeful and a visionary rooted in *holistic* values to bind people together, ensuring the values are understood and operationalised.

Widia endorsed the truth of Jim Collins' statement in his book *Built to Last*—*"If people buy the why, they will manage the how."*

Once people bought into the goal, they were proud to undergo any pain to achieve it.

"Level 5 leaders build enduring greatness through a paradoxical blend of personal humility and professional will."

– **Jim Collins in his book *Good to Great* on Level 5 leadership.**

Alignment Of Purpose and Values

Individual's Meaning

Organization's Purpose

Value Driven Leadership

Organisations that discover the path to greatness by steadfastly adhering to values and larger purpose

Organisations that achieve excellence thro leadership and process but struggle to grow further

Organisations that start well, continue to exist, but don't matter or fade away

CHAPTER 3

Comprehensive Organisation Vision

··

"A clear and crisp vision can stimulate and focus concrete action. The clearer the vision, the more focused the strategy and action. How can there be agreement on the particular steps leading somewhere, if there is no agreement on where you are going? Visions are dreams and hopes that are real to us. They are what we believe must be in place if there is to be a future, and they arise from our most profound experience of life. They exceed our grasp and often seem impossible to achieve. Good examples of a vision are Gandhiji's vision of a free India or Ford's vision of a mass-produced car for ordinary people. Visions are extremely powerful, and they motivate us. When visions are stated objectively, they fuel us with energy and endurance. A vision is not just a picture of what could be; it is an appeal to our better selves, a call to become something more."

– Rosabeth Moss Kanter, Professor, Harvard Business School

Rahul, a consultant with a boutique consulting company, was in an uncomfortable spot. He had some ideas to suggest for his client, but his boss had diametrically different advice. Thanks to this conflict, Rahul was now forced to recommend a strategy that he didn't believe in.

His client, a semiconductor company based in Singapore, needed help to achieve its vision of becoming the market leader. It had set itself a target of 20 percent growth in business and wanted to grow the customer base.

Rahul's boss believed that the only way to do this was by bringing down costs. The company was already operating on scales that would make their products less expensive. Rahul's boss urged the company to automate as many processes as they could and let go of a large number of people on the shop floor. This would get around the problem of the high costs of labour in Singapore. As for the remaining assembly operations that still needed people, that part could be shifted to Vietnam, where labour was cheaper, he said. This seemed the perfect strategy to give the client the cost advantage to compete with Chinese manufacturers.

But Rahul was not convinced. He had a different approach. To ensure the vision of a 20 percent growth and sustain it, the company needed to strengthen its existing customer base, he thought. Cost cutting was not the only answer; sustainable growth was possible only if the company offered an improved product that fulfilled a market need.

"A good strategy would be to invest in R&D to make semiconductors that consumed less power," he told his boss. "These would make the end products more energy-efficient and give them better battery life in mobile phones. As a user, I, for one, would be thrilled to have a phone that didn't run out of charge every few hours."

But he seemed to be alone in his views. There was no support for it from his boss, the client or even the managers in the client company. He completed the rest of the implementation of the project half-heartedly, ensuring that he kept his ideas to himself.

Rahul here had multiple problems. First, there was no alignment between his way of thinking and that of his boss. This difference in approach had created a situation where he was forced to implement something that he did not believe in. Doing something without conviction brought down his enthusiasm levels and did not challenge him to give his best. The conflict itself was rooted in the fact that the client company's vision was being interpreted differently by the two of them; in other words, there was an inconsistency in the deployment of the vision.

Vision statements should inspire to pull the entire organisation in one direction.

While the company vision provides the overall direction for a reasonably long period, day-to-day strategies and realisation of business goals are constantly changing, depending on the changes in the business outlooks.

To meet these business goals, organisations set incentive-linked targets and goals for key people. This often results in a good performance by individuals but not necessarily good overall corporate performance. The attempt to achieve goals set for each individual or function ends up creating what Eliyahu Goldratt, in his famous book **Theory of Constraints**, calls "**local optimums**". There is no alignment of the little islands of individual successes to a common goal.

Sometimes, this kind of polarisation and dichotomy in interest comes from an unintentional divergence of short-term milestones from the vision. For instance, the need to increase profits could be in direct conflict with the need for additional investment in R&D (as in Rahul's case), or cost-reduction exercises might come in the way of sourcing good quality material.

Generally, visions are drawn for a period of three to five years. In most cases, the vision statement is just a transactional declaration relating to what the company wants to achieve. Promises of sustained growth and profit initially bring the organisation and the people together and mutually agreed rewards bind the stakeholders together.

" A limited vision limits.

When the organisation vision is limited to reaching numbers and maximising profits, it breeds a culture where increasing profits is the primary motive, even if it means cutting corners. Concerns such as quality promises to customers and fairness to business associates become a casualty.

Taken to an extreme, this leads to a situation where leaders succumb to business "realities" and challenges, and take the easy way out, even if it is not legal. Transparency, ethics and long-term relationships die a natural death in the race to meet profit margins.

Internally, this translates into disenchantment of people with the leadership and leads to daily conflicts, resulting in an enormous waste of energy, resources and loss of productivity. There is no commitment to a larger cause.

Such organisations win the small battles, are successful and show excellent results in the short term. But will they last in the long run? Is this kind of profit-making sustainable?

It is then the job of the leaders to propagate the vision in its entirety and prevent it from becoming mere words hanging on the wall. They have to think, speak and act in full consonance of the vision so that it is implicit in all decisions throughout the organisation.

For example, does a company that professes to **delight the customer** truly do all it can to solve the customer's problem, even at the risk of seriously eroding the bottom line? Or is the vision abandoned the minute there is a likely adverse impact on the bottom line?

The leaders' conduct is the key to the alignment of the business to the vision. The leader's consistency of actions and predictability sets the tone for the rest of the people in the organisation. People keenly observe the way they respond to a serious problem or a dilemma. If there are inconsistencies between what the leaders say and do, it is only sending out a message of a lack of honesty and transparency. If the leadership is not true to the vision, others in the company cannot be expected to adopt the true spirit of the vision with energy and enthusiasm.

We have seen in Chapter 2 that there are cases when high profile leaders violate the true spirit of the vision to obtain personal benefits or gains, bringing total disrepute to the organisation. This leaves the people thoroughly confused, and expecting them to take the vision seriously would be foolish.

" **Comprehensive Vision is one that encompasses all stakeholders—3Ps**

Visions are usually more long term than business goals. It is like looking at a distant object through a telescope. But the risk of looking through a telescope also is that the field of vision is limited. A company vision that focuses mainly on business-related goals and strategies does not normally include the interests of all stakeholders. At best, it addresses the shareholders' interests in growing business and profits. The expectations of the other stakeholders are normally not met. Visions around 3P include— **Planet** (environment and sustainability), **People** (employees, stakeholders and society) and **Profit.**

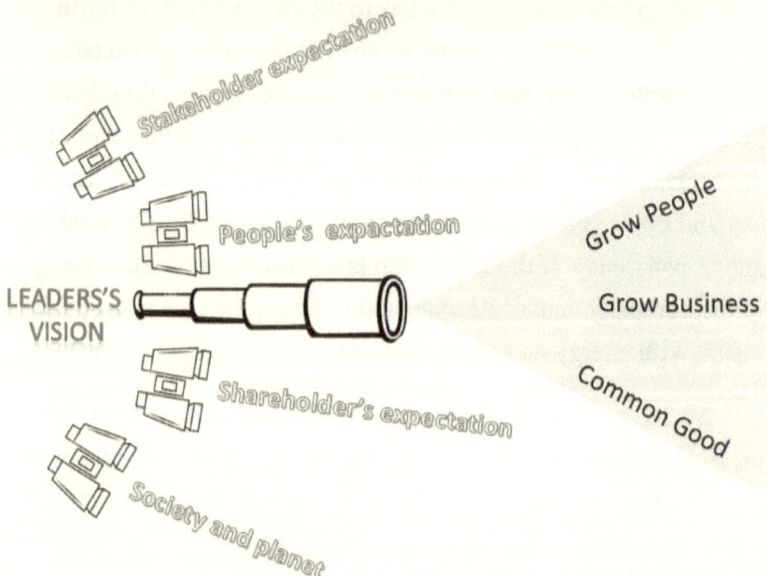

Organisation vision, which is limited to **growing business**, is somewhat telescopic. It needs to become wider to encompass people and the common good.

For the organisation to thrive, grow and excel, the full participation and contribution of all stakeholders (including the critical and most obvious one—the employees and the suppliers) is important. Telescopes can make distant objects appear clearer, but they offer poor peripheral vision. You can only see straight ahead.

A *Comprehensive* Vision* should not only be just farsighted and focused but also wider to include people expectations (*elaborated a little later in this chapter*). In the case of Rahul, he was able to evolve and suggest a sound long-term strategy, keeping product development as the key strategy rather than just reducing costs by saving labour costs. His strategy clearly encompassed the interests of stakeholders—people and suppliers. The boss' strategy would have adversely impacted people and suppliers, sacrificing their participation and leading to detachment from the vision.

> A vision that addresses common good is a vision that triggers excitement and commitment.

A *Comprehensive* Vision* addresses all the stakeholders and motivates people to work for the vision. In turn, they find an alignment to their own personal growth.

Juxtaposing our shared Widia experience with our experience of working closely with a large number of companies (as director on the board, trainer, consultant), we are convinced that these expanded visions, encompassing stakeholders and addressing a **purpose** go a long way towards providing meaning for existence. When people see themselves working for a larger and common good, they bring motivation and involvement to work energetically to meet business goals.

This brings us to the key issue.

Is there a purpose beyond profits?

Can companies answer the question of why they exist?

To arrive at a *Comprehensive* Vision, organisations first need to ask themselves why they exist. Once they understand this, they will be able to expand their visions into a comprehensive one.

Comprehensive Visions are compared with limited vision and explained with these examples below:

Organisation Example	Limited Vision	*Comprehensive* Vision
Power company	25K Megawatts by 2025	We will provide power to 100 million households by 2025.
Automobile company	Produce a fuel-efficient car to reduce the costs of travel.	Provide affordable mobility to people.
Telecom company	Reach one billion households with mobile teleservices.	Allow people to connect to families anywhere.
Pharma company	Bring an affordable cure for oral cancer.	Make life healthier—offer cure without side effects.

Jewellery brand	Become USD 5 Billion in 5 years.	Be the most cherished jewellery brand for women.

To create the **buy-in** and keep the people aligned to the vision, the organisation has to think big, find something that addresses larger and common good that can trigger excitement and enable commitment in the minds of people. **Why** organisations work determines **how well** they work.

A comprehensive or expanded vision needs to include the expectations of the people, other stakeholders like vendors and business partners and, above all, encompass the society and the planet.

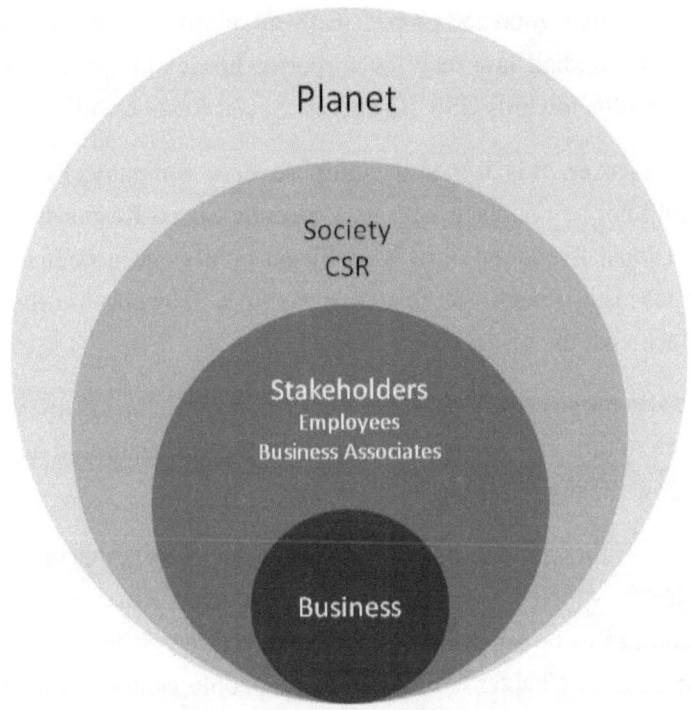

> **"** **Organisation purpose is its reason for existence.**
>
> **All tactics and strategies should ultimately be directed to serving the purpose.**

Today, the aphorism that the "purpose of business is business" has become outdated. Organisations are perceived not as just business entities but as "corporate citizens" with certain social obligations. These responsibilities include ensuring sustainable use of critical non-renewable resources like energy, judicial use of water and materials like wood and proper treatment of effluents and disposal of waste. Indian law requires corporate houses to spend 2% of their profits towards CSR (Corporate Social Responsibility).

However, this is not the purpose of a company. **Purpose** should not be confused with its Corporate Social Responsibility. As Global Branding Guru Alan Siegal points out, a company's purpose is its **reason for existence**. He says, "The purpose should reflect what the distinctive, actionable idea is."

The purpose would be the foundation of **vision** or **mission**, which in turn will be addressed by all strategies, goals and tactics to grow the organisation.

The illustration below explains the *Comprehensive Vision**, which is derived from the *Larger* Purpose. This vision has to be supported by *Holistic* Values, which we have discussed in Chapter 2 and has to be people centric. From the *Comprehensive Vision* flows the strategies and tactics that the organisation adopts. All these tactics and strategies should ultimately be directed to serving the **purpose**.

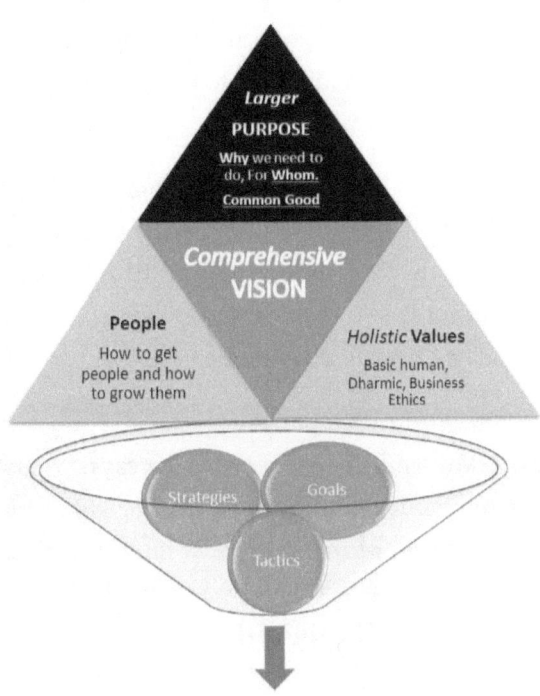

Comprehensive VISION

ALIGNMENT to *Larger* PURPOSE

Companies with the strongest vision statements are those that include a purpose. Some are listed below:

1. ***Patagonia:*** *Build the best product, cause no unnecessary harm, use business to inspire and implement solutions to the environmental crisis. (The purpose is well defined.)*

2. ***Ikea:*** *To create a better everyday life for many people. (The purpose is well defined.)*

The *Comprehensive* Vision statements normally **encompass the three Ps—Planet, People and Profit.**

A strong purpose that addresses a common good and a clear and *Comprehensive* Vision is necessary to give people a clear direction at work and provide job satisfaction. A purpose that is larger allows people to find sense and meaning in their work. The belief that their efforts are directed towards making a difference provides them fulfilment*.

Once **purpose** is included in the **vision** and the leadership creates a culture of support with the people, the quality of engagement and involvement rises significantly. This culture nurtures an attitude of service to a larger common good. A caring and nurturing environment helps people become self-propelled.

The CHRO of Unilever Ms. Leena Nair says, *"I passionately believe that companies with purpose last, brands with purpose grow, and people with purpose thrive in uncertain times."*

People Evolution in Organisations

Organisations and people both evolve over time. What people expect from their workplaces changes with experience and maturity. These expectations may not be articulated but are always present at the back of their minds. The evolution of people in organisations typically goes through four different levels.

1. Physical safety

A fresher merely looks for a good job, an acceptable compensation package and a comfortable working environment. At this stage, they are looking mostly for "physical safety" and comfort.

2. Mental comfort

The next level of expectation is having a role that is well defined, being objectively evaluated and rewarded for performance, having opportunities to learn and grow, and finding a guide or mentor who can provide a sense of direction—all of which contribute to mental satisfaction at the workplace.

3. Psychological comfort

Psychological safety comes from having an environment of trust, where people are free to disagree or point out inconsistencies and are confident of not being punished for genuine mistakes. Not having psychological safety leads to the creation of the "yes men" culture, which can hurt businesses in the long term.

"Psychological safety isn't about being nice," says **Amy Edmondson**, Professor at Harvard Business School, who first identified the concept in 1999. It's about giving candid feedback, openly admitting mistakes and learning from each other.

In fact, Hans Hagemann, Cofounder of the Munich Leadership Group, which combines science with management consulting, has identified the absence of this **psychological comfort** as a key factor in people being disengaged at work.

4. *Psychic* Safety*

Dictionary meaning of Psychic: Relating to the soul or mind—emotional, spiritual, inner safety

This last level refers to a dimension of the human being, which goes beyond the pay cheque and success. It is the craving to be recognised as a complete human being and a capable individual who can contribute and get appreciation. Typically, people in this stage work for reasons other than to just earn money.

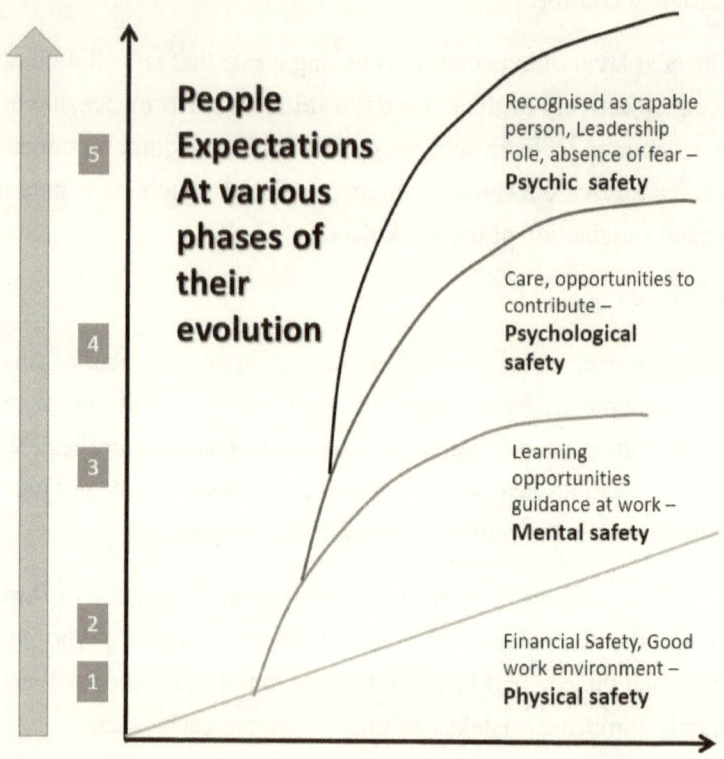

People Expectations At various phases of their evolution

Recognised as capable person, Leadership role, absence of fear – **Psychic safety**

Care, opportunities to contribute – **Psychological safety**

Learning opportunities guidance at work – **Mental safety**

Financial Safety, Good work environment – **Physical safety**

The way that an organisation looks at its people and the way it provides different kinds of safety at different levels in their evolution depends, to a large extent, on how well the top leadership connects with its people. Treating them as a mere **resource** cannot create a *Nourishing* Culture needed to satisfy the four levels of expectations.

People are the prime drivers of purpose and *comprehensive* **visions.**

For the purpose to be realised and accepted, the organisation needs to put people at the core and allow them to be prime drivers of the business. The leadership needs to acknowledge this and create empathy and provide a **connect** between the **purpose** and the people.

They need to provide opportunities for people to contribute as well as to learn. When people contribute, they experience joy and realisation of the **purpose**.

People then become owners of the **purpose**. Problems such as differences of opinion between leaders and the existence of department silos disappear. Each person acts on behalf of the organisation to realise the **purpose**. People become open to ideas irrespective of the source. They are constantly listening and seeking feedback to improve their own standards and provide better service. They question and challenge processes, policies, paradigms that hinder the delivery of the **purpose** and look for better alternatives.

The small contributions made by people have a cumulative impact on the larger cause. It is the intrapreneur mindset, rather than the employee mindset, at work. Engagement is at its highest.

Once the **purpose** is understood and becomes the prime driver of people, volition (the power of using one's will) steps in, and there is no place for command and control. There is active involvement. Contribution itself becomes the reward. No external motivation is necessary. Resources are utilised responsibly. Trusteeship becomes the plank of decision-making. The whole style of management becomes participatory and interdependent. There is mutuality and commitment to do what is right for the institution. Everybody chips in and this has a compounding impact.

This lays the foundation for sustainability. Stakeholders continue to learn and contribute, all the time stretching themselves and their capacity to realise and contribute to the purpose.

On the other hand, when there is limited or no buy-in to the vision, the boss-subordinate relationship degenerates into a contractual obligation. Employees start to look at what they have to do for the salary they get, and the boss develops an attitude that says, **You are paid to do this job, so do it.**

Alignment of people to **purpose** results in:

- Feeling of ownership,

- Equality,

- Empowerment,

- Greater creativity,

- Higher effectiveness, productivity.

 Comprehensive Vision **statement and purpose is also an advertisement— builds a stronger brand.**

As we have discussed before, the best vision statement is that which is comprehensive, has the organisation **purpose** built into it and is centred on people.

The graphic below describes what ingredients are important to make a strong vision statement. A *Comprehensive* Vision is one that not only addresses the 3 Ps but also encompasses growing the business, people and serving the larger and common good as well. If the stakeholders need to be aligned to a *Comprehensive* **Vision,** all these have to be covered. It is, therefore, reasonable to say that a vision is truly comprehensive and well-accepted if it transcends from just including the 3Ps to address what is shown below. People in organisations will align themselves to *Comprehensive* **Visions** more readily than business visions.

It is also very important to understand that what drives this *Comprehensive* **Vision** is purposeful leadership entrenched in values. This we have dealt with in Chapter 2.

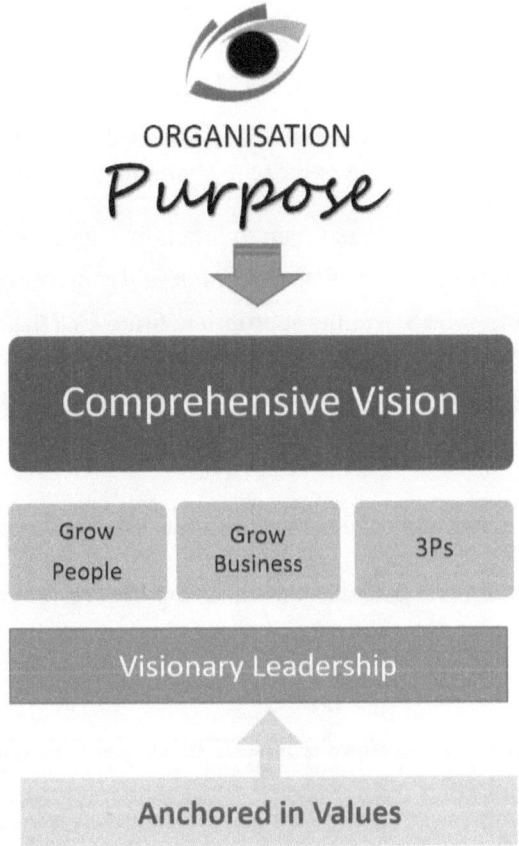

Can leader charisma replace purpose?

There are cases of organisations doing extremely well with business-oriented visions alone and no major focus on values or purpose. This usually happens with visionary leaders who drive organisations with just their personal charisma. They seem to be there at the right time and the right place, and people are motivated by salary and career progression.

Employees develop a sense of loyalty more to the leader than the organisation. This success is there only as long as the charismatic leader is in charge. We have seen many multinational organisations go through aggressive phases of growth, and then start to flounder with the exit of the charismatic leadership.

Startups too have been seen to hit upon a successful business model with the objective of creating value and generating wealth for the founders, who exit at the appropriate time. *Comprehensive Vision*, values and purpose may seem irrelevant to such strategies, but short-term plans are just for the short term and do not work out well in the longer term.

What does *Comprehensive Vision* include?

A vision becomes comprehensive if it has the following aspects included in it.

Purpose – Simple, clearly articulated purpose, which inspires all stakeholders and is easy to relate to.

Business goals – Time-bound goals to enable action planning, derived from the vision.

People growth – Statement on people strategy, enabling them to grow to full potential.

The foundation for the organisation success is heavily dependent on *Holistic Values*, clearly articulated as a combination of **basic human values, dharmic values** and ethics and principles that govern actions intended to achieve the goals.

Vision statements of some reputed organisations are given below. They are all strong visions. We have attempted a little exercise to see how they could encompass the four aspects and become comprehensive. The exercise is simply a way to explain the concept of making a *Comprehensive* Vision.

Apple

APPLE'S VISION

Apple is commited to bringing the personal computing exercise to students, educators Creative professionals and consumers around the world through its innovative hardware software and Internet offerings.
In sum, Apple's vision is to become the "best" at designing and manufacturing electronic devices in the world.

The current Apple vision shown above is centred on the target customers, what they want to offer and what they aspire to be. This vision will become clearer if the "Larger Purpose" is built into the vision. The values and people aspects could also be covered. It is possible that Apple makes separate statements for these.

Comprehensive Vision, according to the authors, is one that is easily deployed and stakeholders can easily connect with.

Apple's purpose and "belief" was…

"To make a contribution to the world by making tools for the mind that advance humankind."

The old belief was:

"We believe that we are on the face of the earth to make great products and that's not changing. We are constantly focusing on innovating. We believe in the simple, not the complex. We believe that we need to own and control the primary technologies behind the products that we make, and participate only in markets where we can make a significant contribution. We believe in saying no to thousands of projects, so that we can really focus on the few

that are truly important and meaningful to us. We believe in deep collaboration and cross-pollination of our groups, which allow us to innovate in a way that others cannot. And frankly, we don't settle for anything less than excellence in every group in the company, and we have the self-honesty to admit when we're wrong and the courage to change. And I think regardless of who is in what job those values are so embedded in this company that Apple will do extremely well".

The old belief of *Apple* refers to the **Larger Purpose**. The values and people aspects may have been dealt with separately.

Ikea

IKEA VISION:

"To create a better everyday life for the many people."

IKEA MISSION:

"Dedicated to giving to the local community well being regarded by our customers and co-workers as a social responsible company."

IKEA BUSINESS IDEA:

"To offer a wide range of well designed, functional home furnishing products at prices so low that as many people as possible will be able to afford them."

IKEA MARKET POSITIONING STATEMENT:

"Your partner in better living. We do our part, you do yours. Together we save money."

The purpose is clear. Ikea strongly targets its customers. It has a service-oriented approach towards the community and can be regarded as a socially responsible company. A strong business and value proposition is driven hard in its tag line and business statements.

To make the vision comprehensive, it could include people and articulate their values into the **vision**.

Mitsubishi Materials Corporation, Japan

All employees sign off their emails with the vision statement, which is given below.

"We will become the leading business group committed to creating a sustainable world through materials innovation, with use of our unique and distinctive technologies, for People, Society and the Earth."

The **vision** is comprehensive—it has a *Larger* Purpose, serves people and planet (larger good) and addresses people.

CHAPTER 4

Organisation Evolution – The Journey to Excellence Unmasked

....

Thirty-five years ago, Sandeep Kothari's father Kantilal Kothari set up a factory to make auto parts for the fast-growing automobile market in India.

For the first 15 years, the company grew quickly. Senior Mr. Kothari put his life and soul into the business. He picked very loyal people to head crucial functions, got consultants from Japan and was almost obsessive about maintaining quality standards. In short, he made sure that the venture was a success.

Much later, as he lay on his deathbed, he had called his son and told him, "Whatever you do, never let the employees and the company down."

When his father died soon after, Sandeep, armed with an MBA from the US, took over the company.

Four years later, Sandeep was a worried man. He had realised soon enough that it was a tough business. With newfound respect, he wondered how his father had managed all those years.

The company still made components for the automobile industry and chugged along, growing at 8–10% annually. But Sandeep was concerned. While the auto industry was seeing unprecedented growth, vendors such as himself were being squeezed on margins.

His largest customer had decided to hold prices and make money with volumes. His OEM customer convinced the parts' manufacturers not to increase prices, promising them more business when the company grew. The OEM did grow, but Sandeep did not get more business because, by then, the OEM had decided to develop more vendors to get better prices and spread its risk.

Frustrated, Sandeep toyed with the idea of selling off the company. On the one hand, he did not want to let his father down. On the other, business was becoming tougher. Chinese and Japanese auto parts companies were setting up factories in India and adding to the competition.

He had other challenges. His key managers, who were much older than him, didn't take his suggestions seriously. They resisted all efforts at modernisation and automation and continued to work the same way as they had in his father's time.

The union fiefdom was strong. Sandeep had tried to bring in a performance-based incentive system but failed. The union wouldn't settle for anything but a mandatory increment of 8% for all every year.

Sandeep's dream of moving into aerospace components manufacture, where margins were better, had yet to take off. It wasn't very difficult to modify the existing factory and machines. The real challenge lay in changing his team's mindset.

His people were suspicious of any change that he proposed. New HR managers rarely lasted beyond six months. The sales and marketing teams were reluctant to sell to new customers. The production team was not geared to innovate. Overall, the company was content to play safe.

To be a successful player called for much higher quality standards and reliability. People in different departments would need to work together. They needed to be skilled differently and become more accountable, more focused, more value-driven and more charged with fire in their bellies.

So far, Sandeep had not progressed much on any of these counts.

Sandeep was caught in a typical syndrome of trying to take an existing business and growing it further. His father had focused on top and bottom-line growth. Once the business model was established and some level of operational efficiency was achieved, the company was content with the profits that rolled in. It had not felt the need for a **vision**, let alone a long-term Comprehensive Vision.

Sandeep's dilemma came from dealing with the culture of the organisation that was formed many years back. To take his company on a journey to excellence, Sandeep would have to make holistic changes to evolve in all aspects.

The good news is that any organisation, at any stage of existence, can still put itself on the path of evolution. This would, of course, require bringing in changes, depending on the phases of growth that it currently is in. To make this identification easier, the various phases are explained below:

1. Starting Phase

Focus is on establishing the business and a little more.

Get things done... limited vision... values are dormant... look for basic competence in people... depend on the leader's style & directions.

The way things are done during this first phase has a huge influence on the future and how individuals start to think. In the first, starting phase of any business, the promoter or entrepreneur has an idea and sets up a team. The emphasis is on getting things done. A dynamic leadership, which monitors and directs operations, provides confidence and motivation to the team to get the business up and running.

The "vision", if any, at this stage is just to establish a successful business and ensure financial stability. There is little time to think about stakeholders, expectations, values and so on.

In this phase, the leader's style and direction are crucial and leave an indelible mark on the future of the organisation.

If the leaders are ethical and believe that the means of business are as important as the end, this becomes the operating style of the organisation. If they show respect for people, they develop a good sense of belonging and ownership. On the other hand, if they are indisciplined and unpredictable, it leaves people unsure with no idea of what is expected of them, and people take no initiative to do anything on their own.

The culture of the organisation is at the embryo stage. But the way things are done during this time has a huge influence on the future and how individuals start to think.

2. Stabilising Phase

Pushing growth... vision is not articulated... purpose is to validate the business idea... stabilise the business... focus on functional competencies

The leadership's attitude is subconsciously reflected by team members and becomes part of the company culture. As business picks up and there is growth in the top line, the organisation moves to the second phase of its evolution. More people are added to the team, which means that it is time to bring in systems and controls. People are hired and groomed for functional competencies, a change from the initial days when teams were small and generally worked together, probably in an ad hoc manner.

The leaders' goal at this stage is to stabilise the operations and the company. Policies need to be put in place. Compensation and pay rises need to be in line with performance.

Once again, leadership values displayed at this stage decide whether the organisation will gain a firm footing or crumble. If the leader is conscious of the need to encourage systematic and proper processes and put in systems that are acceptable by objective standards, the organisation has a bright future. The leadership's attitude to customers, processes and people are subconsciously reflected by the team members and become cemented as part of the company culture.

If leadership is objective in its approach, this becomes the norm in the organisation. However, if what people see from leaders is ad-hocism, inconsistency, dishonesty and undue favouritism and unfairness, they either adopt the same attitude or become disenchanted and leave for greener pastures.

More than words, it is the actions of leaders that demonstrate the values that they live by. Leaders, whose ethics and integrity are obvious in their actions, keep motivation levels of the people high. Generally, people tend to prefer the correct, ethical way of doing things. If they are compelled to act against their own conscience, they feel a sense of dissonance; and no strong team can ever be built on a foundation of conflict and dissonance.

But this phase is also the one most likely to see the emergence of conflicts. As the organisation expands, more leaders emerge with differing points of view, sometimes leading to the formation of fiefdoms.

Apart from that, the leader is often torn between the pressure from the investors and managing the people, between increasing valuations and stabilising financial performance. It requires a display of great leadership to resolve the conflicts satisfactorily and keep the organisation moving forward.

3. Profitable Growth Phase

Improving operational efficiency... looking for functional competencies... growing shareholder value and market size... seeking engaged people... but people are restless and look for more.

Profitable growth phase can be reached, but to evolve further, the organisation needs to invest in people.

If the leadership has been doing the right things in terms of offerings, developing the market and developing internal capabilities, the organisation soon reaches a period of rapid growth and profits.

A large number of mid-sized companies reach this point but get stuck here, unable to evolve any further. Their strategies crystallise around customer acquisition and retention as a part of the business paradigm. Operational efficiencies begin to be challenged. The organisation needs more people, but the investments in people do not seem to deliver to expectation. As more people join the organisation, they bring in their own way of doing things, a different set of beliefs and value systems and a different level of expectations.

This is the phase where the leadership has to start paying attention to details, which may not directly impact the top or bottom line but are still critical in shaping the working environment or the "culture". These include building the right competencies in people, constantly meeting rising customer expectations, understanding changes in the marketplace and competition and encouraging the people within to respond appropriately.

This phase requires people who are highly invested in their organisational roles—something that is possible only when people are respected as important members of the organisation, are empowered and have the freedom to experiment.

If the leadership style so far has been autocratic, with leaders telling people what to do instead of training them and empowering them to do things, it becomes difficult to delegate work, as people have not learnt to work on their own.

If the leaders have been intolerant of the mistakes and have been severely reprimanding people, then it is highly likely that the organisation is purely top driven and people's enthusiasm and energy levels are at their lowest.

Just giving people the freedom to try something new, even if they don't always succeed, helps unleash a huge amount of energy. They feel empowered to contribute towards the goals.

Successful leaders are sensitive to this and understand that people usually want something beyond just a job, position and compensation. They long to be treated with dignity and self-respect and be counted as valuable members of the team. They look for more ways to contribute.

Leaders, who realise that people development is crucial, try to help fulfil people expectations. They also understand that people development extends to employees as well as suppliers, all business associates and partners. They make sure that everyone feels fairly treated and that all are valued as partners.

If the organisation is focused only on business development and growth and neglects other dimensions like systems, processes, controls, people development, it quickly hits a glass ceiling. (Please see Chapter 6 for people development).

When people development is missing, the organisation starts on a downward spiral, sometimes becoming a takeover candidate.

Sandeep Kothari's company in the story stands at phase 3 of the evolution chart. He is caught between the old culture that his father had worked with and his own new, professional approach. His new ideas only confused people, and their engagement with their work dropped. In such situations, the leader has to respond by standing tall, communicating clearly, finding support from like-minded people and developing new leaders who will help the organisation grow.

Sandeep also made another mistake—he had not paid much attention to his father's style of functioning. Senior Mr. Kothari had adopted ethical business practices together with a kind and caring attitude on the people front.

Sandeep, on the other hand, with his Western MBA education was looking at purely business parameters, focusing on margins. He completely neglected ethical and human values, which was probably why he found it difficult to carry his people with him. He was also inconsistent in his adoption of his father's value system; his approach was based on the compulsions of the business situation. Kothari Senior had tried to explain this to Sandeep while on his deathbed, *"Whatever you do, never let the employees and the company down."*

As the organisation reaches a critical mass, success parameters need to go beyond being ethical and complying with regulations. People development becomes critical and needs to be the centre of the organisation's focus.

At this point in evolution, the vision needs to change and grow too. The leadership's views determine the shape of the future of the organisation. Are they satisfied with making money and enjoying the trappings of power and "success"? Do they have a personal vision that goes beyond numbers and shareholder value? Is there a desire to build an "excellent" organisation and the willingness to invest in developing one? The answer forms the new vision and reflects future growth.

Together with the growth in vision, it is necessary for an organisation on the path to excellence to **grow** its people. People growth is defined not only in terms of functional skills but the level at which they are engaged in their work. This is possible when the leader is empathetic to the "psychological" needs of the employees and creates an environment where the basic human values like honesty, integrity, respect and care are part of the organisation values. This culture of psychological comfort encourages greater engagement in the task of building and growing the organisation.

> **Good leaders realise that people make mistakes and are not machines. Having the right people and right leaderships are crucial.**

4. Excellence Phase

Aspire for market leadership... strive for excellence... have business ethics and human values... satisfy all stakeholders... harness potential of people... service driven (CSR)

Providing psychological safety brings out the best in people, creates an environment for all-round growth and an engaged workforce, without which it is impossible for any organisation to reach excellence.

In this fourth phase, where organisations strive for excellence, the biggest challenge is to keep people engaged. Most frameworks of excellence that are currently in use (think Baldridge, EFQM and Deming) advocate getting to the excellence stage through a good vision, strategy, customer focus, processes, technology and partnerships. They recommend strategies to ensure people satisfaction and engagement. They also talk about the importance of sustainability but mainly from the resources and energy perspective.

But our experience has taught us that this approach cannot guarantee truly engaged people. The organisation needs more. It needs to "win the hearts" of people and make sure that they are "psychologically" comfortable.

Nobody can perform to his or her fullest capability if his or her workplace atmosphere is threatening in any way. If the aim is to get people to perform, reprimand and punishment are only counterproductive. Individual competence, domain knowledge or experience needs to be buttressed with **Nourishing Culture*** to "win hearts".

Providing psychological safety by crafting an environment for all-round growth with a climate of appreciation and recognition brings out the best in people. This alone will form an engaged workforce, without which it is impossible for any organisation to reach excellence and stand tall among its peers.

The key to creating this culture lies in the leader's attitude towards people. If the leader treats them with disrespect or does not really value his/her people, no amount of HR initiatives can help. If the leader does not reflect the aspirations of the organisation and the sense of the **vision** in all interactions—meetings, communications and actions—it is impossible to establish this kind of culture. If the leader has no time or patience to invest in developing the capability of his/her people, they end up feeling that they are not valued or seen as capable members of the team. All enthusiasm in their work dies.

The leader could be a dynamic person and may devote a great deal of time and attention to develop and implement the right strategies. However, it is the leader's personal paradigm on people, the strength of belief in ethical and basic human values and conduct vis-à-vis the stated vision that ultimately decides if the organisation can become truly excellent or not.

One other important task for the leader is to constantly measure people satisfaction, identify their dissatisfiers, motivate them and keep them engaged. Very often, this function is left to the human resources department to handle while the leadership is busy with "hardcore" business activities.

When people are engaged in their roles and their work is aligned to the organisation's objectives, improvements take place on a continuous basis, and the approaches to the identified goals are upgraded on an ongoing basis. This allows the organisation to establish possibilities for continuous growth, a prerequisite to becoming an excellent organisation.

5. The Excellent Organisation Evolution Model

Like late Dr. Stephen Covey said everything in the world is created twice, first in the mind of the creator and then in reality. Same is the case of creating excellent businesses and institutions. The ability to envision and act in the direction of the vision is the key to progress and success.

Evolution of organisations could be broken up into four phases and related to three major dimensions. The four phases being start up, stabilisation, profitable growth and, thereafter the climb towards excellence. This progression has been dealt with earlier on in the chapter.

The three major dimensions are the nucleus, enablers and impacted. For purposes of clarity, the three dimensions are broken down into a total of seven sub dimensions.

The nucleus which determines the character, the personality of the organisation is represented by purpose, vision and values. These have been dealt with elaborately in Chapter 2 and 3.

To ensure that the nucleus manifests itself fully, viz., develops to its fullest potential, the leadership, the primary driver of action/ energy becomes the key enabler. On dissecting the leadership as the enabler, one finds that there are two sub-dimensions, reflected in the two pillars, which impact organisational growth/evolution. They are the business paradigm and the people paradigm of the leadership.

The net impact of the enabler vis-à-vis the nucleus affects the evolution of the organisation and its people, hence the categorisation of the last two pillars as 'impacted'.

As the Organisation evolves from being a start-up, stabilizes, gets into a profitable growth mode and thereafter attempts to become an excellent organisation, it needs to evolve along each of the seven dimensions. The chart below captures these aspects along the seven pillars.

The evolution of each sub dimension is explained briefly below:

Excellent Organisation
Evolution Module

	People Expectation Mindset	Organisation status	Vision	Purpose	Values	Leadership people paradigm	Leadership business paradigm
Phase 4 (EXCELLENT)	Aspires a leadership role and intrinsic empowerment	Seeks excellence	3P Vision - Planet, Profits, People & Society	Satisfy expectations of all stakeholders beyond shareholders - ESG (Environment, Society and Governance)	Human values articulated - inconsistency in following	Develop, mentor	To be market leader
	Has achieved success but feels empty	Adhoc support to sections of society/planet - CSR	To be excellent, better than competition, to become a leader and a role model		Values limited to business ethics and compliances	Cares for people	Continually improving processes
	Seeks meaning at work	Deliver better service to customer and stakeholders					
	Wants to have a "say" - expects psychological safety	Harness more potential from people				"Culture fit" overrides "competence fit"	Satisfying all stakeholders
Phase 3 (DEVELOPING)	Is comfortable but restless and looks for more	Seeking engaged people	To grow in size, market presence and make profits	Growing share holder value	Inconsistency in following ethical and basic human values	Willing to train and develop skills	Customer orientation
	Seeks opportunities to learn and grow	Focus on business, profits, less on people				Looks for functional & behavioral competency	Operational efficiency
Phase 2	Wants mental & physical comfort, financial stability	Stabilising phase	Limited to reaching business goals and metrics	To validate an idea and business case	Not articulated / Isolated	Looks for functional competency	Pushing growths
Phase 1	Needs a job and financial safety	Struggling to survive / Start up phase	Limited to day to day results	To fill a percieved void and exploit an opportunity	Dormant	Looks for basic competence / Just a means (resource)	Get things done
	Impacted		**Nucleus**			**Enablers**	

Explanation for phrases in the chart are in Annexure at the end of the book

I NUCLEUS:

This is the DNA of the organisation. It has a tremendous impact on the quality of the personality/character of the organisation. As discussed in Chapters 2 and 3, a vision is time based futuristic perspective of a business outcome. In the normal course, the vision is more about the purpose (what problem we trying to solve, to what extent we would be driving it in a given span of time). Often this also coupled with the how the organisation intends to achieve the purpose and is reflected by the values, which will impact the relationships between stakeholders, quality, finesse of the processes etc.

1. **Purpose** – Purpose changes with the growth of an organisation, from being an attempt to exploit a business opportunity in the beginning and going through phases of establishing a successful business, making profits and creating shareholder and addressing Environment, Society and Governance concerns (ESG) to reach a stage of excellence, where it becomes a market leader, role model and better than competition.

2. **Vision** – This too starts with a primary focus on business goals and wealth creation and then extends to customers who are critical to business. As the organisation evolves, the vision needs to acknowledge the expectations of all stakeholders – people, the suppliers, vendors, partners and the society. The scope of the vision needs to extend to factor in the needs of the society at large, and finally include the planet (3Ps).

3. **Values** – Value systems are dormant at the early stage. Values of ethics and integrity take root for the sake of compliance and later to encompass basic human values, and finally in dharmic values.

II ENABLERS:

The leadership is the key driver for the development of the organisation along the four phases. Like it is said 'Leadership is about everything and everybody else other than the leaders'. The corollary to that is added that, 'ultimately it is the leadership alone as well'. Both these are reflected by the leadership paradigm. It is the quality of the leadership which impacts everything and everybody.

The word 'paradigm', implies, individual 'world view' of the leadership on the particular sub dimension. How the leadership views the vision, purpose, values and seeks to treat the external opportunities to achieve it, reflects the business paradigm of the leader. The vision cannot be achieved without people; hence the leadership's perception of the key wealth creators, the people, i.e., the leadership's people paradigm has a tremendous impact on the outcomes/results.

Given the pressures on the leadership to show growth, revenues, returns etc., it is but natural that the focus on business paradigm is often higher and hence receives maximum investment of time and energy. People who rise to leadership roles bring with them the capability to understand business challenges and develop the right strategies. It is important however that for sustained progress, the leadership develops a strong paradigm around people as well. It is important for the leadership to accept people as they are. Be willing to listen and understand people from their perspective with empathy and take on the responsibility to develop them to their potential. It is important that the people paradigm be impregnated in the mind of the leadership at the initial phases of the evolution.

4. **Leadership, business paradigm** – It is obvious that the Promoter/owner has to drive the business. Initially the focus is primarily centred on business - the leadership's "Business Paradigm". The leadership too has to evolve from somehow getting things done, to pushing growth, bringing in operational efficiency and customer orientation. When the short term goals have been met, the leadership needs to worry about identifying long term goals and make plans around that. The need is therefore for the Leadership to be "visionary". As the leadership matures, it works towards market leadership, ultimately aiming for all round excellence and sustained growth.

5. **Leadership, people paradigm** – This is critical ingredient right from the start. While organisations start, grow and struggle along up to a stage even without this paradigm being right, sooner or later they stumble. Despite having strong business models, strategies, and good hard core business processes, a majority of the organisations hit a "glass ceiling" only because their people paradigm has not evolved to the required maturity. The key is about the Leaders "world view" on people, the acceptance of people as they are, a strong commitment to treat them with respect, care, empathy and a belief that with proper guidance and coaching they could blossom to their full potential.. It is about the leadership accepting that "growing people" is part of the responsibility.

III IMPACTED:

The development of the nucleus gets reflected ultimately in the outcomes/result, of all efforts, resources and energy invested that matters viz., the organisation and the people.

6. **Organization** – The evolution of the organization from just about surviving, to stabilizing, profitable growth and finally excellence is continually impacted by the changes in the other aspects (columns in the chart). All other parameters need to evolve along the lines indicated for the organisation to grow in a balanced way, maturing from one phase to another. If they don't, the organisation's evolution gets lopsided.

7. **People Expectations** – Just like the Organisation evolves in its aspirations, people's expectations also change as they move up in their careers. It starts with having physical and financial security and progresses to mental, psychological comfort. In our experience, one major reason that organisations struggle to get people "engaged" is the failure of the Leadership to understand this dimension of people expectation and address it adequately. The leadership has to understand every stage of expectation and meet it even before it arises. While most organisations meet the financial safety and to a large extent, the mental safety levels, the mismatch that occurs most often is in providing psychological safety. The inability to establish an emotional connect with the people or understand what psychological safety they are seeking creates this gap.

Typically, people who have grown with the organisation and tasted some success are at a point where they look for psychological comfort. When they are unable to find a meaning in their work in view of their limited participation, they feel an emptiness and they look for opportunities to have a say in what is happening around them. Actually what they are looking for is influencing leadership role.

Finally putting it all together, beyond a stage it is just not sufficient to have one strong leader (or even a handful of leaders) with engaged people, organisations need strong leaderships at every level. One leader cannot do it all. The organisation needs to nourish a culture that enables this to happen. The Organisation needs to "grow" people. (See chapter 6 – igniting greatness in people)

Analysing the case of the company Sandeep Kothari inherited from his father with regard to the chart, we can draw the following conclusions:

- As regards the business, the company stands at phase 2, where it is growing and trying to push growth. However, its future is unclear. Logically, it needs to move towards improving operational efficiency and better customer orientation. It needs a good customer-driven strategy.

- The leader's paradigm around people is at a very low level—phase 1. It has not kept pace with the business evolution. They are still treating people as just a resource. They need to focus on people development (covered in detail in Chapter 6).

- The **values** of the company are also in phase 1, which means they are dormant. Despite being in business for 35 years, the values are not clear. People are confused, and hence, they play safe. Fiefdom reigns. Creating a holistic set of values, starting with ethics and basic human values will help people get clarity on decision-making and remove conflicts.

- The organisation has no clearly articulated **purpose** or **vision** of where it would like to reach. There is no common goal to get people working in the same direction. The goals have, so far, been to grow business, improve efficiency, adopt Japanese systems and reduce costs. The organisation has been focused on business profits but has made no effort to get people aligned. At this stage, what it needs to do is articulate a vision that is clear and more comprehensive. Only then the organisation will move to phase 3 and then on to 4.

The organisation obviously needs to get people engaged and harness their potential. The organisation would like to benchmark its competitors who are excellent or market leaders and try to catch up or even overtake them. But bringing in any change can never be easy. To take the organisation forward, there should be a declared purpose. The "purpose" of business needs to go beyond mere profits or creating value for the shareholders. The **vision** needs to become comprehensive to include all stakeholders and the expectations of the society and the environment.

People will not just change unless they see the change happening at the top. It is up to the leadership to develop a *Comprehensive* Vision, evangelise the purpose, and articulate and live the values to bind people.

While all these changes are happening, the leadership needs to be aware of people expectations, provide the appropriate inputs and support as enablers. **Leadership's paradigm** on people also needs to evolve on the lines indicated jointly with adopting the right values.

The chart given earlier maps out the evolution of organisations with regard to the seven aspects mentioned. Looking at it, organisations can get an idea of which level of evolution they are currently at, where they need to go and how to draw up a strategy for further evolution.

Organisations are economic entities. The leadership operates from a paradigm that people are a collection of individual economic units. Propelling, fuelling them with growth, position and profits or money is seen to be the magic formula for mutual success. "Excellent Organisations" have perfected the internal business and people processes to drive these common needs. Most people have fallen for this and permit themselves to be treated as such. Maximising these efforts creates stress, burnouts and takes a toll on organisations and its people. The reality is that people are born 'human' and should not be treated as mere commodities. It is the "purpose", which makes life more meaningful. Life should not be limited to mere economic pursuits.

CHAPTER 5

Beyond Excellence – Leap to "Greatness" "Build an Impactful Business"

··

Lisa Grey ran the India operations of one of the largest US-based software companies in the US. At 50, she was at the prime of her career, successful and had grown her company in India twentyfold in the last ten years.

Lisa was a good manager. She loved working with people and knew how to get the job done. Her good, clear, structured head helped her set up systems and processes.

She frequently met and reviewed her managers and delivery heads. She knew the status of all the projects. She had a good management team, handpicked and trained by her. They were devoted and committed to her ideas and ideology. It had been fun working with them. The entire organisation was run smoothly, much like an army mission.

Things had begun to change in the last couple of years. The company had grown steadily from 200 people ten years ago to 1800 now, with 10 delivery heads and 65 team leads. She still met the delivery heads every month diligently, but she was losing connect with people down the line, the ones who ran the organisation at the grassroots level.

The realisation hit her hard the day she ran into Sameer, a team member and close friend of 10 years. At one time, they met frequently and played golf every weekend. Sameer now came up and asked, "How are you, ma'am?"

Lisa was surprised by his greeting. They had been close associates, on first-name basis. Why was he now referring to her as 'ma'am'? She had set up an open culture and given people the freedom to express their ideas, problems and issues and take pride in finding solutions. What was happening now? Was she losing touch with the majority who were working here? Was the culture changing? And why was it changing when the systems and processes were the same?

'I have to meet our HR head about this,' she thought as she warmly greeted Sameer. "How are you, Sameer?"

"Getting along, ma'am... I mean, Lisa," he muttered. "I have been shifted to head the banking division now."

"Oh, I didn't know that, but I hope you are happy with the change," said Lisa.

She noticed a momentary hesitation before Sameer replied, "Yes, I am. It's new to me, and my team is entirely new. We do well, but somehow, there is no fun anymore." He moved away quickly before she could ask any more questions.

*Walking back slowly, Lisa started getting genuinely concerned. The business and the divisions were growing strongly; people were growing. They were taking on more responsibilities. The organisation's **vision** and **mission** were well-deployed and clear to all. The India operations boasted of the best HR policy, quality policy, ethics policy and had got several accreditations and SCM level 5 certified. She felt people would love to join this organisation, learn here and contribute to its growth.*

So what was going wrong? Lisa sensed that employee morale was low but had no answers why. She was no longer a hands-on manager. She had been slowly letting go, hoping that the managers she had groomed would take over and start running things the way she had been doing. Had the transition not happened smoothly? Would she have to get back to the helm of affairs and start directing things again?

Was the company starting to miss her as a leader? She had thought that the second level of leadership was now evolved enough to manage without having her direct everything.

Why had she not been able to build an organisation that was self-generating?

After business excellence, what next?

Having built an excellent organisation, the question that naturally arises is *'Now what?'* After achieving dimensions of excellence and getting recognised for it, the Baldridge Award, the EFQM Award, the Deming Prize, SCM Level 5 or other frameworks of excellence, what is the organisation's objective? What does it look forward to? Is there anything beyond the mere business goals of growth, profits and shareholder wealth? More importantly, what will keep it running?

If the objective of the organisation and the leadership team is just to keep going, there is not much challenge for the people. Everything becomes a matter of scale. Strategic goal setting, business planning, deployment and managing the organisation goals becomes routine, and work slips into a known and predictively steady pattern.

Organisations, at this stage, are driven by well-defined processes—Standard Operating Procedures (SOPs). In effect, the individual is required to follow the defined process steps and execute the tasks as prescribed. The processes or the "rules" begin to dominate each activity, often pushing the overall objective or purpose into the background. Organisations become bureaucratic and lose the human touch.

Improvement parameters and metrics become incremental. Energy levels drop. There is a feeling of having reached the stage of excellence. There is little incentive or need for creativity. People are not required to exert themselves beyond normal work. Their energy banks slowly get depleted. The fire in the belly disappears. When there is no longer a need to reach for a new goal, things begin to slide.

But is there something beyond **Excellence**? What should the leadership address? How can the organisation ensure that people continue to find work challenging and that there is a continuous flow of energy? What can make an organisation become one that people admire and respect?

The business environment today is undergoing a change in its outlook. Organisations are not only expected to comply with the laws of the land but also to be environmentally conscious in terms of what they produce, how they produce, what resources they consume, the carbon footprint they leave and so on. On top of that, they are expected to do something good for society, specifically, the society in which they operate.

Products and services alone cannot define the organisation. Goals cannot stop with increasing the shareholder value, even if it is done in a responsible manner without harming the planet and environment. An automobile company can no longer be satisfied with being a good or even an excellent car manufacturing company and merely stop with satisfying ESG—Environmental,

Social and Governance requirements. An appliance company cannot be satisfied with making good quality appliances. A bank cannot expect to earn a great amount of respect just because it has processes in place that bring down transaction time.

More and more people today are questioning if the old maxim "to increase the shareholders' wealth" is valid.

The cover story of *Economist,* Aug 24th–30th, 2019, "What are companies for?" proves that even the hard-nosed capitalistic captains of America's large corporations believe that it is not just about shareholder returns anymore.

What are companies for?

According to *The Economist*, a hundred and eighty CEOs of well-known, large corporations in a business round table have clearly stated that shareholder value is *no longer everything.* They advocate equal or even more importance to areas such as investing in employees, protecting the environment and dealing fairly and ethically with suppliers. The Chairman of the World Economic Forum, Mr. Claus Schwab says, "The threshold has moved substantially for what people expect from an organisation." Slowly but surely, we see a movement away from the doctrine of Milton Friedman, which stated, "The social responsibility of business is to increase profits."

There has been a school of thought, for a while now, that believes that organisations must find a purpose, try and ask themselves the question, "Why do we exist?" A deep introspection would reveal a purpose that is beyond profits.

American CEOs have confirmed that it is more than mere shareholder value. They believe that firms need to serve ALL stakeholders and not just shareholders. They need to offer good value to customers, support their workers with training, be inclusive in matters of gender and race, deal fairly and ethically with suppliers, support communities in which they work and protect the environment. Put simply, one could say that addressing the concerns of all the stakeholders, protecting the environment and making profits in a responsible way could be the "purpose". How the society looks at the organisation becomes an important dimension, while drawing up a **vision** and the **strategies** to get there.

It is interesting to note that the European Foundation for Quality Management (EFQM), which has been using a framework for addressing **vision, business** results and **excellence** is now modifying its model where the **"purpose"** gets an exceptional level of importance.

Adopting the right strategies, processes and metrics to protect the planet, initiatives to compensate and satisfy the employees and deal ethically and fairly with the suppliers and partners is fast becoming the new norm.

The overall perception that society has of an organisation has a bearing on the strength of the brand. We see today that customers are not satisfied with merely buying a good, reliable product; they want to buy it from an organisation that they respect or trust. The ideal way to delight and lock in customers would be to evolve into an organisation that they could **admire**. Even the millennials prefer to invest their careers in companies that have adopted a *Larger* Purpose and provide meaning in their jobs.

So for an organisation to be respected and admired in a way that outlasts leadership change and all ups and downs of business cycles, it really needs to go a little further. There could be many different things that society expects an organisation to do, depending on the local conditions and the geographies where it operates. CSR spends by themselves may fail to satisfy the "expectations" of society from a corporate citizen, especially when they are mandatory, as in India.

Earning the respect and trust of customers and society goes beyond being a good corporate citizen, ethical, fair and responsible in dealings. It needs the organisation to find some *Larger* Purpose—a larger "common good" that it could deliver to society.

In the case of individuals, author Steven Covey talks about the importance of purpose, the "true north" to guide them in all dealings. Similarly, the organisation too needs a "lodestar" to show it the right way, a righteous path along which they need to progress. They need to identify something in their own domain that touches the lives of people, makes a difference to them and impacts them positively. This is what we identify as something for the larger common good or a "*Larger* **Purpose**".

The idea of "larger good" is enshrined in the Indian heritage and concept of "dharma", which encompasses doing the right things, doing no harm to things both animate and inanimate, and being true and fair in all dealings. It has been stated explicitly thousands of years ago as the only way to maintain sustainability. This implies that organisations need to develop a strong sense of right and wrong—a sense that is implicit in the code of conduct for the people in the organisation, expressed as values of the organisation (Chapter 2). When values underpin all actions and decisions taken, the organisation can ensure that all actions are contributing, in a true sense, to some common good and are making a difference to the lives of people. The *Larger* **Purpose** becomes the lodestar and guiding factor.

Going back to the Widia example (dealt with in detail in Chapter 2), the company was quick to recognise that its role was not just to manufacture and market cutting tools to the Indian manufacturing industry. It identified a purpose—to improve the productivity of the customers, which turned out to be the *Larger* **Purpose**, making a significant impact on the entire industry.

Purpose

Our purpose is:

To enhance the productivity of industries by being the leader in supplying high technology, quality engineering products and services,

– by being responsive to the needs of customers, employees, business associates, shareholders, the community and society at large,

– through an organisation of committed, highly skilled, motivated and satisfied people striving for innovation and excellence,

and

achieve continual growth in sales and profits through fair means in all dealings.

This became a compelling "lodestar" to facilitate decision-making. The organisation worked with customers to modify their machining processes to improve productivity. This proved to be an invigorating approach, and people at Widia learnt to tackle new and difficult problems with alacrity and confidence, even when dealing with products and solutions well outside the organisation's scope. They came up with innovative solutions without getting bogged down by considerations of commercial viability and helped Widia to build a lasting relationship with its customers.

In today's world of digitisation and artificial intelligence, big disruptions are possible. The need of the hour is for people to work together in strong well-knit teams, identify opportunities and work out innovative new solutions. In the story in Chapter 3, Rahul was seeking a *Larger* **Purpose** for his client, to pursue a path of technological excellence by developing better products to meet future customers' needs in a better way. This strategy would have yielded a far more lasting benefit to his client's end users than just a short-term cost reduction. The absence of a *Larger* **Purpose** for Rahul's consulting organisation was the root cause for the lack of alignment between him and his boss.

However talented the leadership team at the top is, the leaders cannot be the only source of new strategies to sustain organisation growth by opening up new avenues. The challenge for the top management is to create an organisational environment where every member of the team is driven by a superordinate goal or *Larger* **Purpose** to ensure future progress.

Expanding leadership paradigms from *business* to *business and people*.

For such an approach to take firm root in an organisation, the leadership's paradigm needs to expand from business to **Larger Purpose** and develop a new paradigm on people, which addresses their changing expectations and satisfies their own individual search for meaning and fulfilment. They also need to have a strong spirit of service and selflessness.

A transformative leader needs to have a service orientation and want to make a difference in the lives of the people by helping them find meaning in their own lives. The trappings of position, power, money and recognition hold no fascination for such leaders. They need to be truly selfless.

It is also useful to recall the thoughts and words of Mahatma Gandhi, propounded more than seven decades ago. He strongly believed that if one has control over a large amount of resources or money, one needs to think of oneself not as an "owner" but as a trustee, whose behaviour is not driven by greed or avarice. The Mahatma believed that there is enough on the planet to meet everyone's need but not to satisfy their greed. The "trustee" needs to act in a manner that the wealth contributes to a "**Larger Purpose**", to serve the needs of the society, helping people at large.

Transformative Leaders reach a stage of mental maturity where what matters more is to be of service and make a difference to the people within the organisation as well as the society at large (Discussed in Chapter 2). If the organisation succeeds in growing consistently along proper lines, recognition and credit will flow to the leadership as well, earning them a place of pride in the world of business. There is no need to be obsessed with their own "success" as separate from that of the organisation's.

Leaders too, seek meaning in their personal life and career, beyond materialistic gains. People who have been successful in building large organisations and creating wealth often step out to establish a foundation or a trust to help people and society. Bill and Melinda Gates and Azim Premji (Wipro) come to mind.

Does true happiness come only when a person is able to make a meaningful contribution to the lives of others? Is the spirit of service awakened when they achieve a certain level of success? Not really. Because apart from successful leaders, we see people at various levels look for something more than the trappings of power to indicate success.

In the 1950s, the Founder Chairman of Panasonic, Konosuke Matsushita, declared in his book *Not for Bread Alone* that an organisation needs to work for the upliftment of the society. In India, in the early 20th Century, TATA had wanted the organisation to go beyond making steel and work towards "building the nation". Many others (some mentioned in Chapter 3) go beyond mere profits and contribute in a way that offers them a rationale for their existence.

Contrary to business school doctrine, **"maximising shareholder wealth"** or "profit maximisation" has not been the dominant driving force or primary objective through the history of visionary companies. But for this type of thinking to take root, much depends on the culture that prevails in the organisation. For an organisation to go beyond the boundaries of **excellence** and evolve to the next stage, there need to be some pre-existing conditions.

> **The paradigm on business expands, to *Larger* Purpose beyond profits.**
>
> **Leader's paradigm on business has to expand to a new paradigm around people.**
>
> **The leader's value base has to become holistic.**

These conditions bring in a dramatic shift in the way **leaders** perceive their roles. The objective is to become truly corporate citizens who can impact the lives of organisations and people who can impact the organisation and the lives of people around. The leaders' value base, together with a selfless approach and a spirit of service, is necessary to create the right culture.

For instance, the Rotary International's Four-Way Test requires a check—"Is it fair to all concerned?" Strategies and decisions have to be governed by the principle of fairness, and that becomes the touchstone. In organisations with a culture that encourages excellence, decisions should be governed by not only what makes sense for the bottom line but also whether it is in keeping with a "*Larger* Purpose".

The other dimension is the aspect we have already talked about—the way people are viewed and treated. If the leaders' approach to people is to nurture them, give them freedom and space to operate and engage in a participatory manner, all employees are fuelled with energy to contribute their best to **"make a difference"**. No one asks, "What is in it for me?" The working style becomes fluid, cutting across roles and functions. Responsibility is distributed among people, and they contribute without fear. People get a sense of being truly empowered. The feeling of "*Psychic Safety*" enables people to operate with a sense of ownership.

One well-known example of this approach is the story of 3M, which has set itself a target to get 30 percent of sales revenues from new products. People at 3M are known to be passionate about doing something new or solving a problem. The company reportedly asks its employees to spend 15% of their time on solving problems close to their heart, a move that has had a dramatic impact and helped to shape the company to what it is today. This freedom enables and empowers people to work towards finding solutions to many problems faced by them or by people they know—their customers, people at large or even societies as a whole.

3M has perfected this approach and has benefited immensely from it. They are changing and developing products or services to benefit society and are integrating social impact into their core strategies. Many new products are developed by different people, and 3M has mastered the art of exploiting these new products not just to grow the business and make money but also to make an **impact** and make a difference. The organisation is able to evolve to the next stage of maturity beyond excellence to becoming a purposeful, admired organisation by making an impact beyond business.

The leaders' job does not stop with writing down a purpose statement; it begins there. They have to constantly find ways to find a connect between the work people are doing and the *Larger Purpose*—a connect which alone can unleash the energy and the latent potential in the people.

Lisa Grey was leading an organisation that had reached a level of excellence but was still very much driven by business goals alone. As the organisation grew, the excitement and enthusiasm faded away. She was not able to identify a *Larger* Purpose and propagate it across the organisation as an evangelist. People got disconnected and lost their energy and enthusiasm.

The LEAP beyond Excellence – Above and Beyond

In Chapter 4, we had suggested an evolution chart that organisations can use as a framework to evaluate their standing on the seven pillars of evolution. Given below is the chart, which includes the 5th level that is a "leap beyond excellence". At this level, the organisation makes an impact and adds "meaning to people". This is an organisation which is admired, trusted, effervescent and one that stakeholders and society would like to interact or be associated with.

	FULFILLED	IMPACTFUL / EXCELLENT (Vision)	Common Good / Purpose	Values	TRANSFORMATIVE (People)	TRANSFORMATIVE (Impact)
Phase 5						
Acts as an Intrapreneur and makes a contribution finding fulfillment	*Larger Purpose* pervades organisation and governs all decisions overriding profits	*Holistic Comprehensive* Vision - going beyond 3Ps	Serving larger common good - making an impact in the domain the organisation operates in	Ethics, human and dharmic values - *"Holistic Values"* - enshrined in operating values	Fueling a culture of selfless contribution and service and providing *Psychic Safety*	Impact Trancending business
Desires *Psychic Safety* to be self propelled and take on leadership roles					Values people and nurtures	Earning the respect of all stakeholders
Desires opportunities to participate and make a contribution	Clear with why and holistic approach. Rational for existance		Purpose extends beyond shareholder value		Empowering people to contribute to purpose	Functioning aligned to *Larger Purpose*
Phase 4						
Aspires a leadership role and intrinsic empowerment	Seeks excellence	3P Vision - Planet, Profits, People & Society	Satisfy expectations of all stakeholders beyond shareholders - ESG (Environment, Society and Governance)	Human values articulated - inconsistency in following	Develop, mentor	To be market leader
Has achieved success but feels empty	Adhoc support to sections of society/planet - CSR					
Seeks meaning at work	Deliver better service to customer and stakeholders	To be excellent, better than competition, to become a leader and a role model		Values limited to business ethics and compliances	Cares for people	Continually improving processes
Wants to have a "say" - expects psychological safety	Harness more potential from people				"Culture fit" overrides "competence fit"	Satisfying all stakeholders

DEVELOPING

Phase	People Expectation Mindset	Organisation status	Vision	Purpose	Values	Leadership people paradigm	Leadership business paradigm
Phase 3	Is comfortable but restless and looks for more	Seeking engaged people	To grow in size, market presence and make profits	Growing share holder value	Inconsistency in following ethical and basic human values	Willing to train and develop skills	Customer orientation
Phase 3	Seeks opportunities to learn and grow	Focus on business, profits, less on people				Looks for functional & behavioral competency	Operational efficiency
Phase 2	Wants mental & physical comfort, financial stability	Stabilising phase	Limited to reaching business goals and metrics	To validate an idea and business case	Not articulated	Looks for functional competency	Pushing growths
Phase 2					Isolated		
Phase 1	Needs a job and financial safety	Struggling to survive	Limited to day to day results	To fill a perceived void and exploit an opportunity	Dormant	Looks for basic competence	Get things done
Phase 1		Start up phase				Just a means (resource)	

Impacted		Nucleus			Enablers	
People Expectation Mindset	Organisation status	Vision	Purpose	Values	Leadership people paradigm	Leadership business paradigm

A *Larger* Purpose does not imply that the organisation should set out to change the world. It does not also mean that the business goals should be ignored. But it is about finding a way or 'a connect' by which the organisation is able to make an impact and make a difference, either through its products and services or the way it deals with the world outside. The *Larger* Purpose also provides a clue to all those working inside to understand why they are doing what they are doing and removes conflict. This provides a sense of satisfaction for all those working for the organisation and opens up avenues for individuals to obtain a feeling of fulfilment. People should not wake up in the morning with a feeling of being compelled to go to work to get their pay cheques. Instead, they should be happy to do so because they feel like a part of a larger effort to make a difference in the world.

A righteous or dharmic way of doing things has nothing to do with **spirituality.** It is more a question of right and wrong. Our belief is that no one really wants to be part of something "wrong". A work environment that promotes the right way of doing things and does not encourage decisions based on purely profits or margins is usually free of moral conflict. No boss has the moral authority to ask his/her subordinate to go and "fix" issues by cutting corners or making compromises with the values of the organisation. In such an environment, where people have *Psychic* Safety, one could feel absolutely free to blow the whistle if something is found wrong or is in conflict with organisation values and purpose.

In the course of doing business, the organisation must choose policies and actions that do not violate the general principle of right and wrong. It starts with following the rule of the land and the law, not harming the environment and having a responsible policy concerning energy and non-renewable resources. The final important purpose or the dharma is about serving a *larger common good.*

A **Larger purpose**, working for the larger common good, realised through a **Holistic Vision** and achieved with **Holistic Values** are the basic ingredients for an "impactful organisation". This, coupled with the right leadership with a service orientation and focused on growing people will be able to create a **Nourishing Culture** where every individual is energetic and self motivated. In such an environment everyone works in harmony to build a trusted and self-renewing organisation that provides meaning and fulfilment for all. Where Everybody Wins

CHAPTER 6

Igniting Greatness in People

....

We have already established that for an organisation to develop to a level of greatness beyond the levels of excellence, it is absolutely essential that it understands its *Larger* Purpose, the reason for its existence and how it can contribute to the larger common good. We spoke of leaders' role in setting up a value system and driving the vision. But it needs more than just a few charismatic leaders to steer organisations to such self-propelling greatness. It needs several leaders whose potential for greatness has been ignited.

In this chapter, we will deal with how greatness is ignited in people and what kind of organisations have great people.

Great organisations are those that have:

- Great admiration from stakeholders.

- Respect from society at large.

- Trust of the people.

- An environment where people feel fully effervescent and highly energetic and are willing to devote their full efforts to sustain its path of growth and development.

- An environment brimming with energy and activity sustained over long periods.

- The ability for constant self-renewal and self-sustenance and the ability to constantly find new things they can do with aplomb.

- Self-motivated and self-directed people who know exactly what to do in a situation of crisis or dilemma.

- A culture that makes its customers buy their products blindly.

These organisations are able to sustain and self-propel themselves to grow beyond excellence, as shown below:

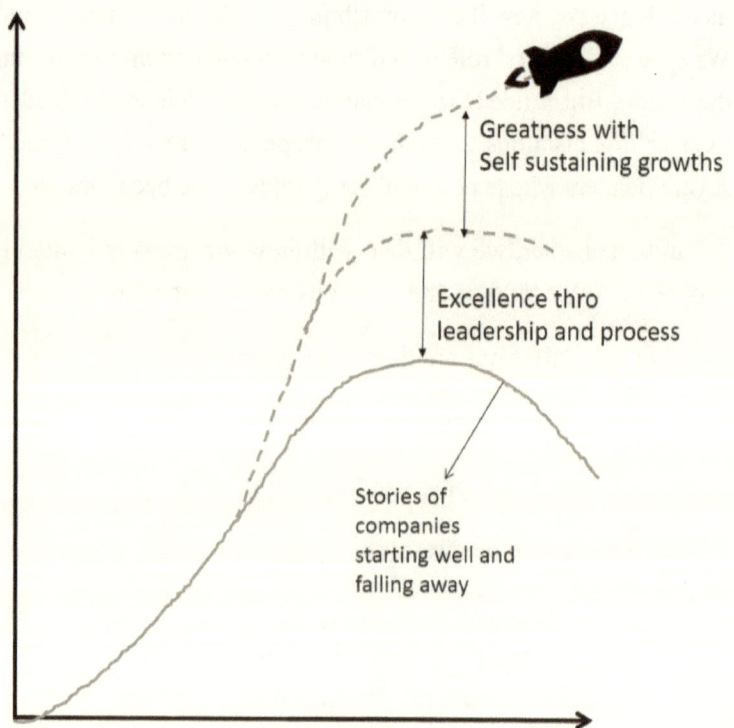

Stop treating people as mere commodities

The first and basic step to making people great is to stop treating them as a commodity or a resource that carries out tasks in a larger system or process.

This mindset is common in many large organisations. They tend to become so strongly driven by the system and the processes that they relegate their people to the background as mere task doers. It is also evident in the terminology too—somewhere along the way, the former 'people/personnel' function got replaced by the cold and clinical 'Human Resources Management'.

With the explosion of interest in Artificial Intelligence (AI), Internet of Things (IOT) and machine learning, the world moves to digital era and a corresponding decrease in face-to-face communications. Consequently, human relationships take a backseat, work becomes transactional, and employees become mechanical and less engaged. HR-led "employee engagement" is reduced to fun and games, managed by event management specialists. The growing number of disengaged people in an organisation is becoming a matter of great concern today.

According to a State of the Global Workplace report, 85% of employees are not engaged or are actively disengaged at work. The economic consequences of this global "norm" are approximately $7 trillion in lost productivity. Eighteen percent are actively disengaged in their work and workplace, while 67% are not engaged.

March 2016, Gallup poll on employee disengagement in the US.

Source: https://www.gallup.com/workplace/231668/ dismal-employee-engagement-sign-global-mismanagement.aspx.. 19/11/2018

> **People evolution and their changing expectations... and leader's paradigm to meet this. Anticipating and meeting people's expectations is a starting point of evolution.**

People's expectations change as they evolve. If the leadership is able to anticipate these expectations of people and provide an environment to meet these expectations, a synergy is formed between the organisation and the people. This becomes the starting point to provide people meaning in their jobs. The conventional leader paradigm, which is usually about business, adds on to include "paradigm around people".

From the chart explained in detail in Chapter 5, we have extracted two relevant columns to explain what the leaderships have to do to provide meaning to people. What is given below are the people expectations in the five evolving phases and what the leadership has to do to meet these expectations.

> **A respectful relationship helps people feel like valued members and not just cogs in the wheel.**

		"Impactful Organisation"	
		Fulfilled	**Transformative**
Phase 5		Acts as an Intrapreneur makes a contribution and finds fulfillment	Fueling a culture of selfless contribution and service and providing psychic safety
		Desires psychic safety to be Self propelled and take on Leadership roles	Values people and nurtures
		Desires opportunities to participate & make a contribution	Empowering people to contribute to purpose
		Excellent Organisation	
Phase 4		Aspires a leadership role and intrinsic empowerment	Develop, Mentor
		Has achieved success but feels useless	Cares for people
		Seeks meaning at work	
		Wants to have a "say" - expects psychological safety	"Culture fit" overrides "competence fit"
		"Developing Organisation"	
Phase 3		Is comfortable but restless and looks for more	Willing to Train and develop Skills
		Seeks opportunities to learn and grow	Looks for Functional and behavioural competency
Phase 2		Wants mental comfort, physical comfort, financial stability	Looks for functional Competency
Phase 1		Needs a Job and financial safety	Just a means (resource)
			Looks for Basic competence
		People Expectation & Mindset	**People Paradigm**
			Leadership
		Impacted	Enablers

Providing an Emotional Connect

In an ecosystem that fosters greatness, the process starts at the very first stage of an employee's life in the organisation—recruitment. When people feel validated as individuals, connected to the leadership and important enough to matter to the organisation, they are already on their way to being ignited.

The organisation recruits people for two reasons—to get a workforce ready for future needs (usually freshers) and to fill vacancies (usually lateral hires).

Fresh recruits are rarely clear about their job roles. The first job is often a plunge into the unknown. Hired for their basic knowledge and skills, the organisation knows that it has to invest time and money to make them industry ready.

When an organisation needs to replace someone higher up in the organisation ladder, it looks for proven competence in the required area and recruits laterally. Often, the emphasis is only on functional competence, especially in the case of parallel recruits whose experience and functional knowledge is very valuable, and aspects like attitude and behavioural competence are often ignored. But whether they are fresh recruits or lateral hires, people at all levels first look for an emotional connect when they join an organisation. It is almost as if they have a board around their neck that pleads, "Please acknowledge me. Tell me that I matter here!"

This emotional connect can only be provided by managers who are sensitive to the employee's emotional needs. When the individual has a qualitatively different, interdependent and respectful relationship right from the first interaction, they develop a good working relationship with bosses, colleagues and the organisation. The individual feels like a valued member and not just a cog in the wheel. It is incumbent on the leadership to create an environment where every individual is treated with empathy, respect and care. This makes every person feel emotionally comfortable and thereby in a position to engage fully and deliver high productivity and quality output. It is obvious that an employee in a disturbed state of mind or with a sense of fear will not be able to perform to their full potential.

By and large, Widia only recruited freshers. Very rarely were there any lateral intakes. The idea was that freshers could be groomed in the organisation culture right from the beginning. At the blue-collar level, selection was influenced by the family background, the need to address critical family responsibilities, sincerity, willingness to work hard and some technical skills. A continuous but consistent message that went out was that taking care of the family was an important part of life. Similarly, caring for the company through quality contribution to the growth was considered essential. These messages left a deep impact on the psyches of the new recruits and remained with them all through their lives.

 Every employee who joined Widia India felt "taken care of", an approach driven by the core value of respecting people and making them matter. Providing means to grow can win the hearts of people.

If the leadership has worked to provide safety and emotional connect, the next level of expectations can be addressed better. Physical needs give way to mental comfort, and people look for ways to grow in the organisation. The organisation can meet this aspiration by reviewing the individual's functional competencies and offering a direction best suited for the growth of both the person and the organisation. By providing this, the leadership continues winning the minds and hearts of the people.

Nobody cares how much you know until they know how much you care.

– Theodore Roosevelt

The focus at Widia was to ensure that people were wholeheartedly engaged and put their body, mind and soul into their work. They learnt principles of integrity, respect and care for people, quality, service and contribution not through lectures but by observing the leadership living out these values. They imbibed the habits of punctuality, professionalism in maintaining commitments, dealing with the toughest of customers and the most sensitive issues as demonstrated in times of crisis. The leadership was truly professional, focused not on profits alone but in the long-term interest of all stakeholders. This made a huge difference. The organisation's interest was sacrosanct.

In most organisations though, the 'on-boarding' process is often restricted to the physical and mental aspects, the real purpose of on-boarding—to create and provide a human emotional connect and help individuals relate their own career and internal aspirations with organisation goals—is forgotten.

Providing all-round training in skills and values win-win for people and their organisation

By now, they have found their area of interest, and they aim to become better at it. This is the stage where people are ready to be groomed to be more efficient. If the leadership complements the thirst for knowledge and desire to excel in the chosen area by providing training and skill development, recognising the functional and behavioural competencies and creating a learning culture, then there is no need to look outside the company for competency.

As Udupa, former Head HR of Widia and co-author of this book says, quoting R. Srinivasan, "If we do not develop our people, who else will?"

Early in its existence, Widia learnt that it was better to "build people" rather than try to "buy" them. This was a lesson learnt when Widia was in the stabilising phase, and the organisation had just hired fresh graduates from top universities as well as experienced talent from other industries.

There was a big expectation mismatch. Widia had planned a growth path for the fresh trainee recruits to work their way up and experience all levels of the value chain, including the shop floor. Graduates from top universities, however, thought differently. The plan didn't appeal to them in their hurry to get ahead fast, and many of them left.

The lateral recruits faced another set of challenges. They had to integrate into a new culture and value system, with unfamiliar operating guidelines and way of working. They started comparing their new workplace with the old one, mixing the two cultures and creating confusion among current working staff. In addition, this trend threatened the dilution of Widia values. It became difficult to get lateral recruits to integrate into all aspects of the organisation that had already been established—the functional, behavioural, operating values and culture.

This led Widia to decide against all lateral intake. Recruitment was done with a lot of care. Often, the managing director and the senior-most managers themselves interviewed the candidates. Only people who clearly understood value systems were hired. Employees would then be moulded into the *Larger* Purpose, the *Holistic* Values and *Nourishing* Culture* of the organisation. The bosses became mentors and took the time to explain things. They were always available to help in case of a problem or difficulty.

Once in a while, a doubt would arise, "Is the effort of training worth it if people decide to leave after being trained?" The organisation had also found the perfect counter-argument. "Is the risk of having untrained people in the company worth it?"

The leadership believed that even if people left after training, they would continue to be ambassadors of the company and provide brand value besides adding to the national talent pool. The ones who stayed back would learn more and grow and be proud to contribute.

WIDIA was committed to providing adequate time and opportunity for learning, based on the firm belief that if the individual did not learn, it was the organisation that would eventually lose.

Provide Psychological Safety

> **Respect people, listen, provide psychological safety.**
>
> **People are likely to perform at high levels when they have psychological safety.**

When people reach a certain level of maturity, having psychological safety becomes important to them. They want the freedom to confront the leadership on work-related issues, voice disagreements about policies and strategies without fear. They appreciate an environment that values fair play, meritocracy, principled governance and absence of politics.

"There is one thing that determines the highest performance, and that is psychological safety—a climate of respect and appreciation."

Hans Hagemann in *The Leading Brain: Powerful Science-Based Strategies for Achieving Peak Performance.*

When individuals are psychologically safe in an environment that includes reward cycles, appreciation and respect, they are highly likely to perform at high levels. There is little need for supervision or instruction, and individual leadership and ownership follows naturally.

Psychological safety is an important ingredient that helps to incubate several leaderships within the organisation. However, the organisation, on its part, needs to establish role clarity and create opportunities for people to get involved and engaged.

Providing *Psychic* Safety*
Psychic Safety is different from other forms of safety.

Before discussing how to satisfy people whose expectations have evolved, we need to understand why people continue to work in an organisation with commitment.

The reason could be one or more of the following:

I am happy with what I am learning here.

I am happy with the challenges thrown at me.

I am happy with the people I work with.

I am happy with the salary and remuneration.

I am happy to grow.

My job is reasonably secure.

Yet more people are leaving organisations after working for 15–20 years than ever before. They are still searching for something. We call that something "*Psychic* Safety".

Psychic Safety is different from other forms of safety. A holistic set of values recognises them as capable individuals, and the transformative leadership gives them the freedom to express their views, to raise questions and operate as an intrapreneur without fear. An alignment of *Larger* Purpose and individual's goals provides a strong alignment. A combination of these creates a work environment that provides *Psychic* Safety.

Organisations that have a clear, *Comprehensive* Vision have identified their *Larger* Purpose and are able to provide *Psychic* Safety and offer people a way to connect the *Larger* Purpose with their own life vision and purpose.

In this kind of environment, people feel that they are an intrinsic part of the organisation and therefore are willing to give their best to their workplace. They rarely think of leaving.

 Psychic Safety at Widia **created genuinely empowered people.**

Widia gave immense *Psychic* Safety to its employees. It started with pride in ourselves as a country and moved to pride in being Widians and individuals.

Why couldn't we be better than the Germans?

Why depend on others when we had strengths of our own?

Why couldn't we offer better customer satisfaction than the competitors?

Why should we feel restricted by the product portfolio?

People asked these questions and were committed to finding answers to them.

Together, they put in their best efforts to find solutions together, knowing their limitations, and also their *Larger* Purpose. This togetherness gave them *Psychic* Safety that allowed them to enjoy what they did and achieve more.

In the initial years, it was a question of survival for Widia that drove it to take on the manufacture of products beyond the planned range. Small teams of people tried to improvise and attempt new things with limited resources. Success was not assured, and the chances of failure were very high.

Still, the top leadership encouraged the people to experiment, supported repeated attempts and was quick to appreciate the effort when something clicked. The production team enthusiastically took up challenges to develop new products. The marketing/sales function was never criticised for bringing in orders that were outside the company's range.

The leadership chose to take these risks partly because the organisation needed to survive. More importantly, it was a demonstration of the leadership's tremendous confidence in the team and encouraged them to persevere in their efforts.

Teamwork became the regular style of functioning. Taking up challenges to work in a new area of technology and create new products and markets that were technologically advanced but unfamiliar was too much work for a single person. By its very nature, it needed the entire team to work on it together.

The culture that Widia had built up was open and transparent. In the face of challenges, people didn't say "It is not my job" or "It hasn't been done before." Instead, there was always somebody who jumped up to say "Let us try it."

Experimentation was accepted as a way of life, and failures were not punished. It was common for people to go beyond their own job boundaries. Some people adapted to this style easily, while others were hesitant. But the reluctance disappeared when they saw how things were being done and the successes that followed.

In a setup where there was no hierarchy for experimentation, where the top bosses did not pull rank or blame people for failures, there was an easy exchange of thoughts and ideas. People were free to walk across to a colleague or a boss, to share ideas to solve problems or suggest improvements to better company performance. People were genuinely empowered. This was not, and cannot be, mandated by a manual. Only organisational culture can determine whether people are willing to take up responsibility unasked.

Dutta Gholba was a Sales Manager in Widia, handling the Pune region. Gholba once visited the factory of one of the prime customers, Telco (Now TATA Motors), in connection with a potential big order. After discussions, the leader of that unit came down to see Gholba and insisted on a discount. Gholba tried to explain that discounts on such big orders needed approval from head office, but the unit head dismissed it saying, "I know your standing in Widia, and I am releasing the order." Gholba made a decision on the spot and agreed.

The next day, he was in a meeting with the managing director and director, sales, for rate contract discussions with Telco and they met for dinner. Gholba was very apologetic as he narrated the previous day's incident. He was embarrassed to have made a decision for a large order without approval.

The Managing Director R. Srinivasan immediately reassured him. "Gholba, it is time to celebrate," he said. "You took a decision in the interest of the company. Besides, your standing with the customer was as such that the top man himself came down to talk. He trusted the rapport between us and gave an order."

Gholba believes that this kind of freedom and responsibility only strengthened his bonding with Widia.

A boss could blame the employee and take the employee to task for bypassing the process. Or a boss could consider the employee's intent and be confident that the employee had acted in the best interest of the company. This makes a huge difference in providing the *Psychic* Safety necessary for people's complete commitment. For this kind of empathy, the leaders need to put themselves into the other person's shoes and understand the situation. At the same time, it cannot be a free for all. While *Psychic* Safety provides liberty, it entails the responsibility not to infringe on the *Larger* Purpose and the *Holistic* Values.

Incubate leaders

The behaviour of the employees is governed by the *Holistic* Values of the organisation. The leader's style of functioning and how they handle tricky and difficult situations set the tone. Are they willing to go the extra mile to satisfy a customer? Are they willing to put aside their personal priorities and find time to engage in finding a solution to the problem at hand? Do they ever say to their functional head "This is your job, and you are paid to do it?" The people observe how the leadership respond to situations and start emulating and imbibing their style. The spirit of the leadership in wanting to invest and grow the people not for strategic reasons but with a genuine intent to develop leaders makes all the difference.

At Widia, the *Holistic* Vision and *Larger* Purpose were very well integrated across the teams. People communicated this with passion and passed on the "contagion" to others.

Achieving the purpose became simple when everyone knew what it was. For instance, if the purpose was "being responsive to customer and driving growth", people did things their own way but always kept the *Larger* **Purpose** in mind and ensured that it was achieved. Being responsive to the customer was the most important thing. Numbers became merely a byproduct.

 Everybody had unambiguously bought into the *Larger* Purpose. They owned it; they had *Psychic* Safety that helped them become leaders.

Widia was made up of many such leaders then. They continue to make a larger difference for common good even though many of them are not working in Widia today.

The organisation became the market leaders and overtook its largest competitor in India in 1988. Thirty years later, Widia (now Kennametal) continues to be the leader in India.

The chart below graphically illustrates the leadership's role in igniting greatness in people to create more leaders.

Leadership PARADIGM

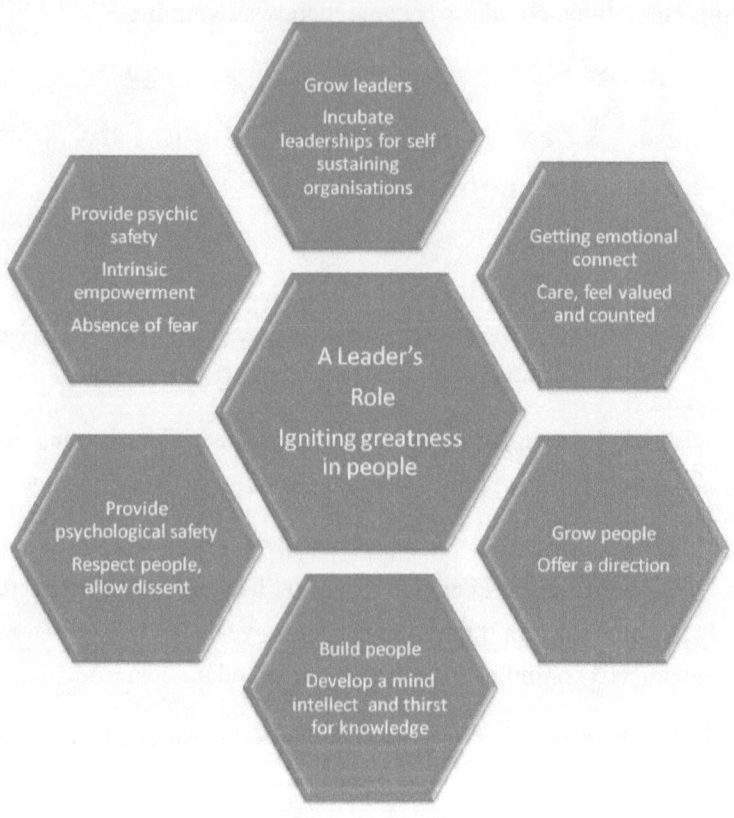

CHAPTER 7

Culture – The Keystone of Impactful Business

"Culture is the smell of a place. It is primarily about people and how they behave."

It is difficult to precisely define the "culture" of any organisation. The late Professor Sumantra Ghoshal called it the "smell of the place". Culture is the outsider's first view and experience of an organisation. It is the way an organisation carries out its business and deals with its employees, stakeholders and partners. It is the emotional connect that makes sense of employees belonging to the organisation that they work for. This has a significant impact on the individuals' behaviour, which collectively forms, becomes the organisation's conduct and culture.

A visitor to an office or a factory gets an immediate taste of the culture of the organisation depending on whether they are either met with helpful staff and pleasant replies, or chaos and unreasonably long waits.

The first thing someone walking into an organisation notices are the people. (The other things are usually inanimate—like furniture, machines, visual merchandise and the decor.) The person's first experience with the organisation depends on the conduct of the people, which is a product of their belief systems and values.

It is easy to form an opinion based on the dominant spirit in a group, their interactions with each other, the way they talk to their bosses, whether things seem organised or chaotic, whether people look happy and confident, and whether they respond with enthusiasm and sincerity.

As interactions increase, other aspects of the culture become apparent—attitude to customers, the quality of the product or service they deliver, their attitudes regarding meeting commitments and keeping promises.

A combination of all of these tells us how well things are done.

The "spirit" of the organisation indicates the engagement levels of the people and whether they really enjoy what they are doing. In short, culture primarily has to do with people and the way they behave. Most important, it has a serious bearing on the outcomes of the business.

> **Culture is influenced by how you treat and get treated by people. Is it a top-down process?**

In any workplace, the culture and the tone are set by the leaders and the way they behave in day-to-day transactions and make decisions.

"*Yatha raja, tatha praja*" goes the Sanskrit saying, meaning, "As the king is, so are the citizens". The leader is the king of the organisation. If the leader uses his/her position to exude power and authority and displays arrogance, the next level mirrors his/her attitude and operating style. The same behaviour flows down the hierarchy to the lowest level employee. It spawns a command and control culture, where fear dominates, and people can never be free and open.

> The *Larger* Purpose, the *Holistic* Values and how the leadership views and treats its own people lay the foundation of great organisation culture.

Once the people paradigm of the leadership is in place, each employee is transformed into a partner. People see the leadership working towards a *Holistic* Vision based on *Holistic* Values and serving the larger common good, rather than being just business result oriented. When the leadership believes in the saying "*Sarvejana sukhino bhuvanto* (may everyone be happy)" and cares for the safety, wellbeing and growth of all, all the people develop a strong belief in it and become a part of the *Larger* Purpose and common good.

The *Larger* Purpose is a unifying factor, binding together an organisation and its people together. The more powerful, broad and inclusive the purpose, the easier it becomes for people to identify, find meaning and relate to it. The *Larger* Purpose creates a oneness, enabling people to find meaning, fulfilment in contributing to the goal and valuing their ability to make a difference in a spirit of selflessness. Collaboration is at its best with everybody co-creating to achieve goals. As people are filled with energy, there is no need for external motivation or incentives.

Leadership people paradigm shapes the culture of the organisation.

Culture influences behaviour. Behaviour consistent with organisational values reinforces the culture.

There is an interesting story of an Indian and a Japanese driving down an empty street early one morning in downtown Tokyo. At a junction, the traffic lights turn red, and the Japanese stops his car.

Surprised, the Indian points out that no one is around, so it doesn't make sense to stop. It is the Japanese's turn to be surprised, "How can I drive through? What if a child is around somewhere watching us breaking the rules?" he asks, a possibility that is horrifying for him.

People behave in a way that is moulded by their culture. In 1995, after the Kobe earthquake in Japan where approximately 6000 people died, citizens stood in an orderly queue. Each person bought grocery that they needed for just one day, ensuring that there was no hoarding, and everyone got something.

Compare this with a culture where stores go empty during a calamity because everyone selfishly races to hoard. The shopkeepers themselves hoard supplies to sell at steep rates later.

The way people behave reflects the culture. For instance, when a father dropping his young son to school zips through a red light just because no police officer is around, he is unknowingly teaching a certain type of behaviour and passing on a culture to the next generation. The child is absorbing a new lesson—that breaking rules is the smart way of reaching the school on time.

If the father does get caught jumping the traffic light and responds by slipping some money into the hands of the constable, the child has learnt another lesson—if you get caught, just buy your way through.

This is the classic, subtle way in which culture is ingrained. Repeatedly watching a certain kind of behaviour makes it the norm.

Brought up in a culture like that, the son behaves similarly in all other situations—cutting corners and bribing people—to get admission to educational institutions, get a job, to avoid paying taxes.

The same behaviour is carried to the workplace. People are trying to outsmart each other to become rich, famous and successful at any cost. We lament the country's lack of ethics and extol the virtues of other societies. We blame the government and politicians for all the evils in society, forgetting how we are systematically poisoning our culture by our behaviour day in and day out at the workplace and in society.

Just as the combination of soil conditions and the environment determines which variety of flora and fauna will flourish, the social environment determines the kind of people who will grow and prosper. Luckily, the right social conditions can be consciously created and nurtured by elders, seniors, leadership in institutions and organisations.

The evolution pillars that influence culture in organisations

The three aspects of evolution, which primarily affect the culture in an organisation, are:

- *Larger* Purpose—How people are aligned to this.

- *Holistic* Values—The combination of ethics, human and dharmic values that bind people together.

- **Leader's paradigm around people**—How the leaders think, speak, act and behave and how people are treated.

This *Nourishing* Culture is graphically represented below.

The three main aspects illustrated above that shape the culture in an organisation depends on how the "human spirit" is nurtured within the organisation.

The organisation, on its part, has the right leadership, *Holistic* Vision and strategies. It is able to progress on its path of evolution from being just a profit-making organisation to an excellent one and leap beyond excellence where it becomes an **impactful organisation where everybody wins**. Such an organisation can outlive its leaders and founders.

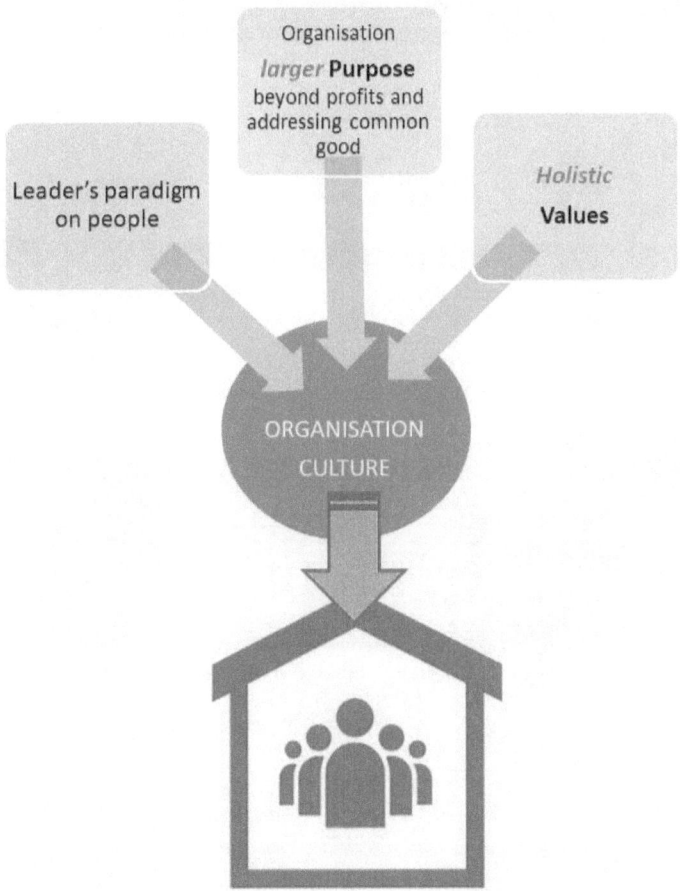

"When you combine a culture of great discipline with an ethic of entrepreneurship, you get a magical alchemy of great performance."

– Jim Collins in his book *Good to Great*

CHAPTER 8

Making a Difference

···

The Widia Culture – the Collective Subconsciousness

In an old and often related folktale, three stonecutters take three different approaches to the work. For the first, his job of cutting stones is a drudgery, which he must do to earn money for survival. The second thinks of it as a means necessary to take care of his family. The third looks at his job as a work of devotion and sees himself helping build a temple.

The perception of the task changes even a hard, exhausting one into a labour of love. The point of view from which people operate determines the quality of effort and, therefore, the outcome.

Siva Subramanian (SS) was one of the first employees who joined Widia in the newly formed Special Purpose Machine division. His division had to supply the first machine to Ford Tractors. The assignment came at a slightly inconvenient time—SS was about to get married. Still, he believed that he could finish the installation and take time off for his wedding. But there were more challenges on the site than he had anticipated. There was no support from the customer. He had to work long hours to complete the installation. No transportation was available when he returned from work late at night, and he had to hitch rides on oil tankers and trucks. The installation process was not yet complete, and his wedding day was near. SS took a short break to get married and came right back to complete the installation.

The story of this extraordinary commitment from a young engineer to complete the job was something that even his bosses didn't know—until 35 years later when he posted it on WhatsApp.

There was no pressure from his bosses or the customer to make personal sacrifices to complete the job within a deadline. SS set himself a very high standard of excellence to ensure perfection beyond what the customer expected. He explains that it was the Widia culture that drove him. He underwent great personal inconvenience even though no one would have grudged him some time off for his wedding. SS' action, in retrospect, could be described as 'selfless' service. The reward for the inconvenience and effort was the satisfaction of making a difference to the customer.

Going back to the stonecutter, what prompted those different kinds of behaviour in the stonecutters? A question that follows is, 'Is it possible to influence the thought process and, therefore, the behaviour of people to reflect the same attitude of service as the temple builder?'

Usually, organisations leave behaviour to chance. Corrections are made on the fly. However, great leaders realise that it is both risky and expensive to leave things to chance or try to change people behaviour with a few classroom sessions. The only way to ensure consistently appropriate behaviour is through the process of etching and embedding it through repetition.

Given the right ambience and experience, behaviour can be learnt and replicated. Lessons learnt through experience become part of our subconscious and sensitise us to the right kind of behaviour. With repeated reinforcement, it is converted into a habit and becomes 'spontaneous'. The behaviour of people is a reflection of the collective subconsciousness—the organisation culture. The predictable response, promise and the delivery becomes 'the brand'.

Temple building is a metaphor for the organisation's purpose or the 'why' of its existence. When the *why* is answered, there is an inspiring purpose for people to relate to emotionally. All effort is directed towards the purpose, and this results in the satisfaction of having made a difference. The larger and clearer the purpose, the easier it is for people to relate to it. The bigger the impact of one's actions, the greater is the intrinsic motivation. The purpose needs to be relatable, and an extension of the business the organisation is engaged in. Each person should be easily able to see the link with his/her own work, talent and career. Only then will people find some meaning in the work they are engaged in and find it fulfilling. This is what we have referred to as the *Larger* **Purpose**.

Great leaders believe it is possible to provide necessary experiences so that the behaviour of the people in the organisation becomes predictable and consistent.

They also recognise that everyone has some element of greatness and the potential to contribute to becoming a "temple builder" instead of remaining a "stonecutter". It is possible to provide specific learning to mould behaviour in patterns that become predictable. It is also possible to tap into people's potential and help them realise it fully. Building a temple of any kind requires multiple sets of skills, and it is possible to nourish and nurture the latent talent and greatness embedded in people to bring out the best. The first step would require getting the lodestar right—identifying the 'why', the 'temple' and the *Larger Purpose* serving common good that the organisation wishes to pursue.

The Widia story followed a similar path. Though it was not explicitly articulated, leaders were aware very early in the journey that:

- Widia was a great opportunity to contribute to the productivity of the Indian industry and thereby contribute to the wealth and growth of the nation.

- Indians were second to none and were fully capable of coming up with solutions. This potential needed to be nourished and allowed to flourish.

- People formed the most important element to meet the organisational purpose and, therefore, needed to be respected, valued and treated fairly.

The perception of the why determines the how.

Understanding the "why" of the business brings commitment and discipline and provides an unending source of inspiration and energy.

Every business meets a need in society, but what makes organisations stand out is their perception of the 'why'—the main reason for the business to exist. For instance, Johnson and Johnson's tagline 'We are in the improvement in the art of healing' or Disney's statement 'We are here to make people happy' clearly spells out the reason for the existence of the company and the entire organisation is devoted to that purpose. Once the people understand the spirit of the business, executing the organisation's plans become easier and better. People are not exchanging labour for money or working to feed their family but to make a difference to the community.

It is the duty of the leadership or the 'supervisor' to provide a *'Super Vision'*—serving a *Larger* **Purpose**, which will change the perception of the people in the team. By "living the culture", the leaders can demonstrate a passion bringing a deeper, subtler and more profound perception to the team members. Understanding the "why" of the business brings commitment and discipline and provides an unending source of inspiration and energy.

Only people who feel valued can create value.

The Widia leadership treated the union as a key partner.

The Widia culture acknowledged every individual's capability and potential, making each person feel valued. This prompted people to seize every opportunity to create value for the customer and the organisation. People were constantly nurtured, encouraged and prodded to tap into their potential to provide innovative solutions.

> Everyone is a temple builder. Union leadership was partner in progress... creation of a unified vision... *Larger Purpose* and common good

The Widia India Employees' Association was formed in the early days to address anxieties around the security of employment, mental and financial safety. The leadership treated the union as a key partner and constantly urged it to overcome vested interests and look at decisions from a long-term and sustainable perspective. Union representatives were appointed on boards of bipartite bodies such as employee housing society, welfare committee, sports committee. They were treated as custodians of organisational resources and welfare of the people.

Widia even had a common vision workshop for 15 union leaders and the top leadership at Widia to help carve out the future direction of Widia and a strategy to get there. The attendees agreed that the growth of Widia meant that all stakeholders, employees and their families would benefit. Very interestingly, the only thing that the union leaders asked for at the workshop was a good school for their children. It was this aspiration that led to the formation of Widia Poornaprajna School in 1987.

You can't take Widia out of Widians

A very senior person from a well-known conglomerate once told R. Srinivasan (Former Managing Director of Widia and one of the co-authors of this book), that Widia had produced more successful

CEOs and directors than many larger companies. This comment set him reflecting on what it was about Widia that it created so many leaders.

Srinivasan believes that whatever happened was neither planned nor designed. The magic happened organically. Ex-Widians who swear by the magic that holds them together even after thirty-odd years came forward to share their experiences and thoughts. All of them continue to lead, taking with them the Widia culture and attitudes wherever they go. Sharing their thoughts on this magic, they spoke about the Widia culture of making a difference and how they continued to do so.

Chitra Phadnis writes based on her interview of Widians:

If the Widia philosophy and approach ever needs validation, it comes in an overwhelming rush from people who had worked there between the 70s and 90s and beyond, after it was taken over by Kennametal. Ex-Widians reliving experiences through stories that were over 25 years old.

Despite being very busy people in senior positions heading various organisations, they all found time to reminisce and share their thoughts. In a telling measure of their affection for their old company and leaders, they carved out time on Sundays, on holidays, late at night, on their way back from work and just after a hectic overseas business trip.

"Even if you call me at midnight, I will be happy to speak on this subject," said Mr. Watson, putting into words what the others hinted at.

As a principle, Widia of those days had recruited mainly freshers straight out of college or people with a couple of years' experience. All of them trained with the company, learnt and imbibed the culture and are continuing to keep it alive today. Interviewees described the culture as "infectious", "encouraged by the leadership" and "part of the people's DNA". Taking pride in it, ex-Widians continue to follow the culture in their current places of work, building "little Widias" wherever they are.

At Widia, people worked hard, often at the cost of time that they could spend with the family. A lot of them felt that "it was not like work at all". Another observation that came through the interviews consistently was the support of the family at home. The family not only supported the Widians; they also took great pride in being associated with the company.

Today, a number of ex-Widians are in very senior positions in the industry—heading Multi National Corporations (MNCs), large Indian corporations or are entrepreneurs who have set up their own businesses. The impressive number of CEOs from Widia has itself been a source of amazement to people in the industry.

Here is what old-timers at Widia had to say:

L. Krishnan joined Widia in the year 1982 as a graduate trainee in sales. He worked for 15 years in Widia and later became the CMO of a large Indian group before he took on the responsibility of Managing Director of TaeguTec India (a Berkshire Hatheway group). He has also been **President of the IMTMA**—Indian Machine Tool Manufacturers Association and Chairman of the Confederation of Indian Industry, Karnataka Chapter.

"Widia was a high-learning organisation, not so much by design but as its way of operation. With minimum support from the collaborators, the company was driven to be innovative and creative and become a market leader in India. It took upon itself the task of improving the customer's productivity and, thereby, established a sound and lasting relationship. The organisation was continuously trying out new ways of doing things to solve customer problems in its domain.

The level of freedom to try out things and experiment was very high. The environment urged us to 'attempt something, even if didn't always work'. A very important legacy that Widia gave was the belief that failures should never stop us. This taught us, as individuals, to never to take no for an answer—a great lesson etched in us. Another important aspect was the access to management at all levels, including the senior leadership that even the new recruits had.

When you get exposed to that culture in the early part of your career, it becomes part of your DNA. It shapes the character and way of thinking. Wherever we go, we carry this part with us. I don't consciously bring it, but this is just the way I operate. Managers in Widia demonstrated and communicated the culture very well. They all walked the talk."

* * *

P. Ramadas joined Widia in 1984 from Hindustan Machine Tools, which was a large government organisation making machine tools. He joined as a manager of the newly formed SPM (Special Purpose Machines) division.

Widia was like a "gurukulam" for us.

"Widia was a moulding place. Overall, it was the Widia experience that made me capable of starting a venture. I follow similar principles in my current company, my second startup with a turnover of Rs. 6.5 Billion, 1500 employees and 750 vendors.

I like to believe that my company has given 2500 people a happy life."

Today, he says that he has the same value system in his company.

"We are a 100 percent ethical company, with no tolerance for bribes—things we learnt at Widia. The focus is not just to make money but to understand the customers' problems, provide the right solution to improve their operations and the living standards of people working for us, and those working with us as vendors. We try to help the society at least in a small way. Widia was like a "gurukulam" for us—it gave us an all-round development and a great experience that I can never forget. Not being afraid to experiment or fail was ingrained in us. We took a lot of risks and tried new things. Failure was never questioned, because of which we became successful. Work ethic, integrity and value system was there for all to experience and follow."

At Widia, I grew from fearful to fearless.

* * *

Hari Prakash joined Widia in 1990. He worked for 10 years in several sales functions and left Widia after heading sales as Regional Manager. **He is the CEO of Gulf Petroleum,** handling a sale of over 100 Million USD. He was earlier the Head of Asia for Castrol, based in China, controlling China, Asia and Australia.

"What drove us those days? It was the leadership, which was par excellence, driven by passion and sound value base. Nothing was impossible. Success at Widia was not a one-time thing; it was continuous. We set audacious goals and went after them. The sort of training that we underwent was something unique to Widia. What a customer visit was like, visiting the shop floor where the action was. It made us confident. A can-do attitude was instilled in us.

We were encouraged to meet the CEO/MD of the customer company even though the tool that we were selling was just 2–3 percent of the customer's spend. The Widia purpose of improving the productivity of industry drove me to explain how a small tool could help to make or break their profits. That was the difference. Then my customers were willing to listen. It raised the profile of Widia in their eyes.

Even after I left Widia, a visit to the shop floor became a part of my ritual. A small suggestion to change a tool at times became the basis for an emotional connect. Replicating some of the practices that I learnt at Widia helped me make an impact even on large customers, who would otherwise have never given us the time of day."

* * *

M. S. Krishnan joined Widia as one of the first graduate engineer trainees. He worked in Widia for more than 25 years. M.S. Krishnan was later the Vice President of Harita Grammar Limited and President, JBM Group, both large auto parts manufacturers in India.

"Keep your eyes and ears open. Listen to every sound and understand what it is. 'If something does not look right, don't just pass it by; ask, clarify or set it right' was a very important lesson that we were taught. And keep looking for improvement. To this day, I follow these two fundamental principles in my work.

It was more important to find out 'why' something went wrong, rather than who made the mistake. The system and environment never treated people as just a pair of hands but always as human beings with a capacity to think. They were repeatedly asked to think about what they were looking for. Qualities such as humility and punctuality were held high.

At Widia, no learning was out of bounds. I just had to ask people and learn. Even now, when I narrate stories from Widia to other people, they are surprised at the amount of freedom that I had to poke my nose anywhere I wanted—in the organisation's interest, of course. Even my wife says there can be nothing like Widia. We used to work till late at night, but I had full support from the family.

Once, we had an 83-day strike, which was a bad experience. On the day the people returned to work, R. Srinivasan told us to welcome everyone back the same way, even the ones we knew had thrown stones. We religiously followed the instruction, and the people were surprised and asked why we didn't react differently. They were told then that if they wanted something, they just needed to ask. Those days, we were like a family—MD to worker.

When I took over as a Vice President of a large auto parts manufacturing company, and I needed something, and I went myself to see the person who could help me. He was busy working, so I waited until he finished.

When he looked up and saw me, he was very flustered, 'Why didn't you call me, sir? I would have come,' he said.

To me, it was the most natural thing to do; after all, I was the one who needed help. Much later, he told me that something like that had never happened in the company before. Even managers summoned others to their office, and here, the Vice President was coming to him to get some work done. The bottom line is that at Widia, the company touched people's hearts."

* * *

P. R. Mujumdar joined as a sales engineer and rose up the sales hierarchy, moved on to lead the TQM and business excellence programmes. He spearheaded the Widia Business Excellence process to apply and get the recognition from CII. He then moved on to Batliboi as CEO, SPM Division. Later, he took on the role of a Business Excellence Assessor for the CII–Exim Business Excellence Award and has completed assessments of over 30 large organisations in India and abroad.

"The all-round training, grooming gained in all organisational functions, as well as the strong value system, and the way leadership treated the people were of immense use in my subsequent assignments. I regularly share my learnings at Widia with companies I assess, and they benefit from the perspectives and practices followed at Widia. Widia was a relatively small company, but with its focus beyond only profits, on basic values, commitment to people and other stakeholders made it a role model.

Some of our senior people were top class people. Having seen other companies, I see now how they groomed people. All of us in sales had a manufacturing or engineering background. We were trained to engage with the customer at all levels. We were also encouraged to interact with the MD of the customer company and find out trends in the industry. Widia was a small company but a role model.

In my current role as an assessor of business excellence, this all-round view of all aspects of the manufacturing sector stands me in good stead.

* * *

B. C. Rao joined Widia in 1983 and is on his third stint in Widia (now Kennametal India). For the last three and a half years, he has been the Managing Director of Kennametal, India.

"When I joined in 1983, what I enjoyed most was how we worked as a family. I was struck by the feeling of connectedness and the humility of leaders and the kind of empowerment we had. The environment then at Widia is one that we know today as the 'startup culture'. We could experiment, fail and keep exploring.

As an individual, I learnt to listen to the customer closely. Widia was the true hallmark of backward integration—we extended all services that the customer wanted and earned great trust and respect. The Kennametal management too recognised the startup culture and the customer intimacy that Widia had built. I must thank the Widia leaders who continue to be there for the blend of old and new—traces of old Widia are still present. I can still see a lot of Widia in pockets. Today, across the globe, the focus is on collaboration, cost improvements, customer, pride in your job—concepts that Widia practised for decades.

Widia was a unique organisation; there was professionalism with a personal touch. It saw success not just as a company making money but also created several happy families and happy, responsible, contributing citizens."

* * *

P. Srinivasan joined Widia as a graduate trainee in the year 1979. He worked in production and headed a plant in Widia for 15 years. He is the President in the large Motherson Group (sales over 6 Billion USD) heading more than 8 companies across different verticals in India, Spain, Egypt and ASEAN.

"The operating values and the senior leadership at the helm were responsible for the culture that emerged in Widia. One of the first things that helped was the recruitment process itself. Most of the new recruits were youngsters straight out of college. The importance of acquiring basic skills, being hands-on, working on machines and dealing with people was drilled into everyone. The new recruits experienced the culture and imbibed the value system. Very few companies give grassroots level culture exposure that we got at Widia.

The youngsters practically grew up absorbing the ideas that Widia believed in. Once they had been moulded, the next thing was to hold on to these people to continue the culture with single-minded devotion. This was very crucial, and the leadership handled it in a way that made all the difference. The leadership was dedicated and hands-on; this encouraged and motivated the people.

More than anything else, treating everyone as human beings, the operating values at Widia, the bonding and relationships made the difference. The elements learnt then are a part of me and my style now. All ex-Widians heading various organisations are trying to build little Widias in the places they are in now."

* * *

Purushottam joined Widia in 1974 as a machine operator. He left Widia in 1995 and established his company 25 years back. As a small-scale entrepreneur with 60 colleagues in his company, he caters to the very special tool requirements of many large Indian and multinational companies. He is a proud entrepreneur and has won the Karnataka State Award for Small Scale Industries.

"I rejected several job offers just to continue working with Widia. They were unique. I was especially impressed by R. Srinivasan's personality, way of handling and maintaining relationships, and his humanity. I have tried to adopt all his values in my own career as entrepreneur. My company spends over rupees two lakh on education for the employees' children, we organise family annual days, and whenever any of them faces a financial or health problem, I apply the same Widia approach to helping them. Whatever I am today, I owe to the great experience and knowledge that I gained in Widia. I am practising all the things I learnt in Widia for over 21 years. I have tried to adopt these values all through my career. I owe my current status to whatever I learnt in Widia. I am now encashing the benefits of great experience and knowledge."

* * *

S. Chandra Mohan is currently Chairman, CII Tamil Nadu and Group President, Finance and Investment, TAFE, part of a 5 Billion USD group, which makes engines, farm vehicles and implements. He interned in Widia after his chartered accountancy and worked for 20 years in Widia.

"My Widia experience moulded my career and life. It strengthened my ability to explore and navigate beyond my function and look beyond numbers. Widia helped us develop a holistic personality. We worked together, and all departments were aligned to a common goal in the interest of the company.

These days, people talk about Steven Covey's *Seven Habits*, but these habits were something that Widia followed long back, around 30 to 40 years ago. Widia treated everyone with respect, as human beings, and had a unique and rare camaraderie with the union as well. The leadership never behaved like 'the entitled'.

When I left Widia, it was not a big company. The companies that I moved to were large, but I could still manage very well. I had gained confidence in Widia to be able to work with any assignment. The Widia culture had given me good exposure and experience to be able to do that."

* * *

Suresh Kannan was in the internal audit department at Widia. He is now the Manager and CFO of Meta Helix Life Sciences (A TATA Enterprise) He says:

"The most important lesson I learnt in Widia was that the finance person need not always agree with the MD. I learnt at Widia to do the right thing, even at the risk of losing my position. The leadership always stood for principles, and these were ingrained in me strongly. My fundamental strength was based on my experience in Widia. In subsequent organisations, it helped me withstand pressures and gave me the courage to go to the management and say that something was wrong.

Proximity and emotional connect with employees was a hallmark of Widia leadership. Being very high on principles, there were no compromises on ethical issues. This was in the 80s when corporate governance and ethics were not really common.

The Poornapragya-Widia School was an idea of the leadership to provide quality education to the children of the employees and from the community around the factory. I am a very proud parent of that school. My son, who studied there, went on to do an MBA from London. The school ensured high class, value-based education for children of employees at all levels. Welfare activities at Widia took care not just of the people but also their children's lives in the future."

* * *

Watson joined Widia at the time of its inception in 1967 as a toolmaker.

"At Widia, we never felt the burden of time or work. There was nothing that we didn't do. The exposure we got to all aspects of the work was very good. Widia encouraged risk taking. No one ever got ticked off for failing; they only got pulled up for not trying.

I attended training programmes that built my capabilities as a supervisor and later as a manager. The leadership used to spot potential and drive people to do their best. I worked there for 40 years and retired as the Vice President.

Patiently, they would explain why it was important not to take shortcuts, to do things the right way even if they were difficult. People were trusted, and trust was wholehearted.

We often discuss those great days. For us, it was like a big family; it was never just going to work and coming back.

When R. Srinivasan left, a big loss was felt. My team in the Hyderabad plant began to ask me questions. 'Will the same culture continue? Will we be able to talk as easily to the MD as before?' and so on.

'As long as I am there, leave it to me,' I assured them, determined to be a 'mini R. Srinivasan'.

After retirement, a Malaysian company wanted me to head their Pune facility. Here, I see opportunities to apply things I learnt at Widia in all aspects of management. From a loss-making situation, I have been able to transform this division to be the best among the seven divisions worldwide."

* * *

Sunil Taneja joined Widia in 1980 as a graduate engineer trainee fresh after his Bachelors in Engineering. He had a six-year stint in Widia as a sales engineer, after which he was bitten by the entrepreneurial bug and left Widia. He created a company with Swiss technology from scratch. Today, he proudly heads a 500-strong people-centric organisation and successfully exports very high technology products to the most advanced countries of the world like Germany and Japan.

According to him, "The culture in Widia was fantastic. Some very good mentoring ensured that I could find my right way forward. Whatever I learnt there—the principles and the way to approach business-related and people issues—are the foundation on which I have been able to create my own successful company. We set very high-quality standards, and this enables us to export to technologically advanced countries.

Widia was the first and last job I ever held before I turned entrepreneur. Over the years, I have seen the working of many companies closely. I have yet to come across a parallel in terms of culture to that of Widia. The whole team was working towards a single purpose.

At a recent meeting in Shimla, he recollected R. Srinivasan's advice to him as a trainee. 'Try to find a purpose in what you are doing,' the MD had said. It was this statement that prompted him to reflect on his life and this, he feels, seeded the spirit that eventually led him to set up an immensely successful company.

* * *

V. Aswatha Ramaiah is presently a trainer in management and has trained over 500,000 people.

"For most of us, Widia was our first job—we were starting on a clean slate with no hangover from earlier work cultures. We learnt everything exactly as it was taught. We were trained and tutored on domain-specific, professional skills as well as values of life, and soft skills. Widia looked after the people and developed them in a comprehensive manner, giving opportunities for growth at the physical, mental, emotional and social levels. The culture sculpted our personalities.

A high level of emotional connect characterised the relations between the workers and the executives. The Widia School was an expression of that organic emotional connect; it channelled the sense of belonging. The workplace took on a family tone. The openness and transparency, value systems ensured that the work environment was totally professional. Everyone could communicate, differ on issues. Discussions were free and frank without any fear of retribution.

"One aspect of Widia emerges clearly and vividly. The quintessence and basic substratum of the passion of Widians was to align to the *Larger* Purpose of humankind. All the transactions taking place at the ground level (amongst the Widians, between Widia and its customers and the myriad stakeholders) could be traced to the transcendental purpose of doing good to the industry and people. This genuine longing to help people (through the industry) was the fuel which propelled every Widian. Achieving impressive financial parameters, incredible innovations and enviable image became incidental or even just byproducts of this obsession to the dharma (righteousness) of making the peoples' lives more worthy of living and the organisation a delightful place to work.

There is no training I have done over the last three decades, which did not carry the flavour, spirit and essence of my learnings at Widia.

The culture of Widia could be summarised as 'People are the prime movers.'"

It is beyond doubt that Widia turned stonecutters to temple builders.

The three important ingredients to build a strong organisational culture were an intrinsic part of Widia. There was a *Larger Purpose* or the guiding lodestar, a holistic value system that laid equal emphasis on human values and dharmic values, and all of it stemmed from a strong leadership whose people paradigm made all the difference.

Let us see the writing on the wall

Let us identify the *Larger* Purpose

Let us practice *Holistic* Values

Let us **Ignite Greatness in People**

Let us build an **Impactful Business where everybody wins**

Impactful Organisation

An organisation which rises 'Above and Beyond' mere shareholder wealth and excellence to make an impact and serve a larger common good and earn the admiration and trust of the wider society.

Impactful Organisation: An organisation which has been able to clearly articulate a *Larger* **Purpose** to serve the common good. Where the vision and strategies are derived to serve the *Larger* **Purpose** and make an impact in the domain it is operating. Where the leadership anchored in dharmic, basic and ethical values recognises the need to "grow" people and succeeds in creating a nourishing environment. An environment wherein people, energetic and enthusiastic, put in their best efforts as if the company belongs to them and work for the sustained progress and provide increasing levels of satisfaction to all stakeholders.

Creating Impactful Business

Disruptive Environment

Business leaders are slowly realising that they may have got it wrong. Getting everybody to be enthusiastic about business goals and working in unison is increasingly becoming a bigger challenge. Visions are too narrow, skewed in favour of the shareholder. Shareholder wealth creation is being chased for far too long now.

Business leaders are just beginning to see the writing on the wall. The 20th-century maxims, "business of business is business", "business is for profit" do not hold water anymore. The refrain from the days of the Baby Boomers and Gen X fail to attract, impress and engage Millennials and Gen Z.

Solving a problem or addressing an issue in society to make money is passé. The existence of business is to solve a problem, aimed at the betterment of society. Business also needs to be conscious of the environment. The means becomes an end in itself. Profit at this stage becomes a corollary, a reward for making the process of delivery more efficient, effective and not the driver.

Leadership Quality

Sharing profits is opportunistic; sharing of ownership of purpose is an opportunity. Not creating ownership in the heart and minds of people can be ill afforded. It is the responsibility of the leadership to make it happen.

Millennials and Gen Z are not willing to be led by leadership, which has the scarcity mentality of the Baby Boomers. For them, survival was an issue. The mentality was to grab everything possible at any cost (grab licences, scarce resources, conniving to create entry barriers, etc.). Nor are they buying the theory of profit maximisation of Gen X (who were driven by ambition, power, profit, even at the cost of exploitation). Today, survival and comfort have been provided for by parents and grandparents.

The current generation does not want simply to be "unit of economic value add". They want to work for organisations, which extend ownership of the cause. They want to work for organisations, which extend ownership of the cause and the opportunity to serve a larger need in society. The organisation and the leadership need to be committed to it.

Leadership Style

Humans' quest for meaning has been in existence from time immemorial. Happiness, peace with oneself, is a state of mind reached through contribution and making a difference. The same continues in today's world. Organisations are also living entities and, therefore, are not any different. People get distracted with many things during the life journey and get stuck. Can organisations afford to get stuck with only increasing profits? Resources belong to the society. Is the leadership therefore not obliged to serve a larger common good? It is the onus of the leadership, therefore, to ensure that the organisation does not get paralysed in any way. They have to evolve and contribute to society. The leadership needs to perceive institutions as resources belonging to the society. They need to see their roles as trustees, therefore utilise the resources for the benefit of society in the best possible manner.

Normal business relationships are contingent between all stakeholders inter se. Cooperation is only to the extent of overlap of mutual self-interest. In an impactful organisation, purpose and values create a stronger bond. The leadership is about adding a bit of *Larger* Purpose, compassion, the spirit of service into every transaction creating the magical transformation, co-operation to co-creation. People own the purpose and, therefore, look at influencing and impacting through the depth or breadth of results expected.

The organisation and leadership need to passionately serve the purpose and create conditions to get the commitment of the people. The individual should feel that the organisation provides a platform, an opportunity to influence how delivery to customer can happen and thereby impact society.

The Organisational Culture

The culture should enable people to evolve through the Maslow's hierarchy, transition people to actualisation, enabling *Larger* Purpose at the earliest. This requires leadership to believe in and encourage investment in the growth of people. It is the responsibility of the leadership to nurture the people, provide the direction, help them discover life goals and enable achievement.

Further, the leadership creates an atmosphere devoid of fear, where people willingly make themselves vulnerable, take risks, experiment and also take the liberty could question the intent and actions of those leading the business.

Respect, care, compassion and willingness to serve a common good form the foundation of relationships. The atmosphere is collegial. Hierarchy exists in structure; however, leadership relationships reflect more of equality than equity in transactions.

Right People

Having the right people on board is critical for the success of any institution. The renowned author, Jim Collins, said "People who buy the why will manage the how." The leader and, therefore, the organisation, will get people who are attracted by the larger value proposition to society and not for the money paid and position offered.

The leadership needs to look for the right people who look at life as an opportunity and with values in congruence to that of the organisation. The current generation goes by inner strength and courage of their conviction. They have whatever is required for a comfortable life, often coupled with the added luxury of their own home, luxury of cars, etc.—all provided for by parents and grandparents. Throwing crumbs no longer is going to buy engagement or commitment.

Career is seen as an opportunity to create an impact on society. It is not about vertical growth, transactional power and money. Career is about making choices, getting a canvas where the contribution is what matters. Life is invested in challenges, which provide meaning and opportunity to make a difference. Career is no longer a drudgery but journey undertaken with devotion. What is invested is love of labour.

Results

Impactful businesses automatically create the right brand. The name provides the promise; the people behind the organisation ensure delivery of promise in letter and spirit. In impactful organisations, the *Larger* Purpose becomes a mass movement, which galvanises people. People become a congregation and not a crowd or a part of headcounts. **People are not stonecutters but temple builders.**

Life as an Opportunity

Each of us too, as leaders, can transform our business, organisation, profession by focusing our energies and resources on meeting the needs of society, as a movement, and not continue to pride in being a juggernaut for profits alone!

Businesses provide us with the opportunity to leave footprints on the sands of time. Are we willing to invest our lives for the *Larger* Purpose?

– Shrihari Udupa

Plaint of a Corporate Lifer

I sit at work; my computer, a blur;

Alone I plod, it is difficult to breathe.

I tried to work hard and smart... but still, I suffer.

This work is evil—'tis not suited for me.

Along comes the boss, with all his profound advice

It makes sense to some, but never, never to me.

No spirit, no zest is his to give—

Fame, glory and money are all that he likes to see.

We had once aspired to lead and inspire.

We had no inspiring people to look up to, but this was the say,

"Finish the task, the job at hand, do what you may,

Do what it takes. Earn your pay and go on and away."

We lack a vision, a purpose, a lodestar, a pilot

To steer us, to guide us, to put us to the test.

We are confused, frustrated, and now we are stressed

To be better than the others, better than the best.

Is there a way, is there a company, is there a nest?

Can there be a place, which brings out your best?

Is there a company, which is better than the rest?

Has it got the stuff to sustain and reach the crest?

Is excellence enough, or is there a higher pinnacle?

Are there purposeful people enough to lead and build?

Above and Beyond, we need to leap,

To BUILD an IMPACTFUL place, where everybody is FULFILLED.

– Mukund

Glossary

....

The following words marked with an * are used in the book with a specific meaning in the context of this book and are explained below:

Purpose:	Purpose in an organisation's context is "why it exists". Normal purpose is to exploit an opportunity, build a successful business and make money. It addresses the expectations of all shareholders.
Larger **Purpose:**	*Larger* **Purpose** in our context means what common good the organisation is serving, beyond merely creating wealth for the shareholders. The *Larger* **Purpose** then becomes the lodestar to align all activities. When choices are made, the test then becomes "Does it serve the larger common good?" In short, *Larger* **Purpose** beyond profits.
Vision:	Vision generally captures what the organisation would like to be at a future point in time. Commonly limited to business goals and focused around shareholder value.

Comprehensive Vision	The two words used in conjunction refer to an enlarged vision. *Comprehensive* Vision expands the business vision to address the stakeholder expectations & 3P—Planet, People, Profit.
Holistic Vision:	Used together, this term captures the purpose of the organisation and serves a larger common good. *Holistic* Vision relates to making a difference to the players in the domain they operate. Corporate Social Responsibility (CSR) activities come out of the profits made (2%) whereas the *Holistic* Vision influences the why and the way the organisation functions and profits are made.
Larger common good:	Larger common good is going beyond the 3Ps and making a difference and impact in the domain the organisation is operating in.
Physical safety:	Providing base-level expectations of the people-compensations and work environments, largely addressing the physical expectations and needs to provide a sense of "physical" safety.
Mental safety:	Providing clarity on roles, responsibilities, expectations and opportunities relating to job requirements, providing training and inputs to improve capabilities. It is about providing a sense of "mental" comfort.

Psychological safety:	Extrinsic empowerment, being treated with respect and care as a human being and getting an emotional connect with the organisation, providing an environment to have a say in related matters.
Psychic Safety:	Having a feeling of being intrinsically empowered and to operate with freedom, and without fear as an intrapreneur. Freedom to question and debate and speak out when something is wrong.
Holistic Values:	This is a word that the authors have coined, which embraces apart from the business ethics the basic human values and the Dharmic values. Please see Chapter 2 for more details.
Nourishing Culture:	A culture, which is necessary to build an IMPACTFUL organisation. Please see Chapter 7.
Success for individual:	Accomplishing goals and achieving material success—like Pay, Position, Esteem and Career.
Meaning for an individual:	As an individual evolves, the person seeks meaning beyond "success". Finding a connection between the work and the larger common good provides meaning. Fulfilment comes from making a significant contribution.

Impactful Organisation:	An organisation that rises "Above and Beyond" mere shareholder wealth and excellence to make an impact and serve a larger common good and earn the admiration and trust of the wider society.
What is Dharma (Organisation context)?	The word "Dharma" is used in this book in the context of the organisation. It relates to how the organisation achieves its *Larger Purpose* by choosing to follow a righteous path. Dharmic acts will be sustainable.
What is spirit of service?	It is a dharmic principle, "less of me" and more of the larger common good. Spirit of service requires underlying selflessness in all actions, decisions and general conduct.

ANNEXURE

Explanation for Phrases Used in Evolution Chart

PEOPLE EXPECTATIONS	
Phase	**Explanation**
Phase-1	**Needs a job and financial safety**: When a person enters the job market, what they look for is merely an opening, a job in a reputed/good, well-known company at a decent compensation, or financial safety.
Phase-2	**Wants mental comfort, physical comfort, and financial stability**: Seeks physical comfort at work. Wants mental comfort—job must improve knowledge base, looks for answers to their questions and thereby learn new things. Wants to earn more as his/her wants increase.
Phase-3.1	**Seeks opportunities to Learn and Grow:** Looks for role expansion, growth and responsibility, expects the organisation to support in his/her personal development.

Phase-3.2	**Is comfortable, but restless and looks for more**: Once employees are financially stable, comfortable in his/her workplace and also learning and growing, the daily grind (monotonous work) does not seem to satisfy them. They feel empty and disengaged, want some meaning in the work they are doing.
Phase-4.1	**Wants to have a "say" – expects psychological safety**: Individual looks for identity, acknowledgement and recognition as an important member of the organisation—an emotional connect. The pay cheque alone does not satisfy him/her. He/she expects to have the freedom to question unclear decisions and have a say in matters connected to them. Looks for "Psychological Safety".
Phase-4.2	**Seeks meaning at work**: He/she starts looking for something beyond the materialistic benefits, career growth, position, authority, etc. He/she looks for some meaning in the work he/she is doing and a connect with his/her own life goals.
Phase-4.3	**Has achieved success but feels useless**: Has achieved a measure of success in his/her career. Seeks alignment between his/her growth expectations and organisation ability to provide for the same. And in the absence of the same, he/she feels "that he/she is wasting his/her life" and feels "empty".

Phase-4.4	**Aspires to a leadership role and intrinsic empowerment**: Wants to participate in decision-making. They look for empowerment so that they can proactively contribute. They want to be respected and valued. Wants to take on leadership roles and responsibilities.
Phase-5.1	**Desires opportunities to participate and make a contribution**: Looks for opportunities to freely express ideas, thoughts in areas beyond the realm of work. Keen to expand their canvas. Wants to contribute in a proactive manner.
Phase-5.2	**Desires *Psychic Safety* to be self-propelled and take on leadership roles**: Would like to question the status quo, without any fear of reprimand. Looks for freedom to creatively engage and make a difference within the organisation.
Phase-5.3	**Acts as an intrapreneur, makes a contribution and finds fulfilment**: Money and career success do not seem to provide satisfaction. Need full empowerment to act as an intrapreneur within their "sphere of influence", make contributions, achieve something and find some meaning and fulfilment.
ORGANISATION	
Phase	**Explanation**
Phase-1.1	**Startup phase**: The main effort is to demonstrate the "proof of concept" and find resonance from stakeholders. Finding and putting together the right team.

Phase-1.2	**Struggling to meet ends**: Find avenues to manage cash burn, become cash positive, manage expectations of investors and people.
Phase 2.1	**Stabilising phase:** Stabilising operations and revenue stream, bring alignment and buy-in from the management and operating team.
Phase-3.1	**Focus on business and systems, less on people**: The focus at this stage is primarily on business numbers and results. There is hardly any time or effort to understand what people want and address related issues.
Phase-3.2	**Profitable growth**: Getting the business and operations more organised and strengthen the base on which the business rests. Focus is on the customer, product development, costs, supply chain and sustained profitability. Focus limited to business goals and growth.
Phase-3.3	**Seeking engaged people**: While core leadership is committed to business, the challenge is to provide motivation to all the people and keep them engaged. Better salaries, perks and packages are offered to try and "buy" people. Also trying to manage attrition through lateral hires.
Phase-4.1	**Harness more potential from people**: To improve competitiveness, the need to tap into the potential of the people starts to gain importance. Increased efforts to develop people and build capabilities.

Phase-4.2	**Deliver better service to customer and stakeholders**: The strategies aim not only to provide better products/services to customers to enable growth but also to take care of needs and expectations of other stakeholders like own people, vendors, partners, etc.
Phase-4.3	**Ad hoc support to sections of society/planet – CSR**: The strategies address not just business needs. Initiatives are taken to mitigate the impact on environment. The Corporate Social Responsibility is recognised, and resources are allocated to address some of the needs of the society.
Phase-4.4	**Strives for excellence**: Focus on processes to become better than the nearest competitor and then aspire to be best in class in all aspects of the business.
Phase-5.1	**Clear with why and holistic approach**: Rationale for existence. Find and articulate clearly the "The rationale of existence", the "purpose" and align the **vision** and strategies to be in sync with the same.
Phase-5.2	**Purpose pervades organisation and governs all decisions, overriding profit**: Developing a sense of service for a larger common good. Wanting to make an impact or a difference. This sense of purpose pervades the organisation and governs all decisions and actions.

VISION	
Phase	**Explanation**
Phase-1	**Limited to day-to-day results**: The vision is mostly not articulated, and the thinking is limited to prove the validity of the idea. The actions and efforts are to make a successful business case.
Phase-2	**Limited to reaching business goals and metrics**: Merely implement the business case and achieve the matrices and business goals.
Phase-3	**To grow in size, market presence and to make profits:** The vision is limited to business goals. Vision is only to grow the business and create shareholder value. The other stakeholders are, at best, a dot on the screen.
Phase-4.1	**To be excellent, better than competition, to become a leader and become a role model:** The focus is to become excellent by focusing on all business processes to get sustained results. To become better than competition, be a market leader and a role model industry. This becomes an ongoing process to seek unmatched size, valuation or excellence.

Phase-4.2	**Comprehensive/3 P Vision—Planet, Profits, People and Society**: A clearly articulated vision, which goes beyond business, results to cover customer, people and society. There is a strong focus on customer satisfaction and people satisfaction. The vision also expects compliance and being ethical in all its dealings. The impact on environment has to be addressed, and sustainability also becomes a requirement. The expectations of society also become relevant.
Phase-5.1	*Holistic* Vision – **Going beyond 3 Ps**: The **vision** needs to be holistic going beyond business, and aligned to the purpose of the organisation to serve the "identified common good". The strategies and tactics must all be governed by the overarching purpose. This impacts "**how**" the leadership and the people go about doing their job.

PURPOSE	
Phase	**Explanation**
Phase-1	**To fill a perceived void and exploit an opportunity**: When a business starts, the purpose is limited to identifying a business opportunity and exploiting the same.
Phase-2	**To validate the idea and business case**: Test the idea and business approach, demonstrate the same and seek validation from the shareholders (investors, owners).

Phase-3	**Growing shareholder value**: Once the idea is validated, the "purpose" shifts to profits and building shareholder wealth.
Phase-4	**Satisfy expectations of all stakeholders beyond shareholders—ESG (Environment, Society and Governance):** The purpose extends beyond merely creating wealth to understanding and meeting the expectations of all the stakeholders—employees, customers, vendors and partners and even the society at large, besides fulfilling all aspects relating to governance. Today, the term ESG (Environment, Society and Governance) is gaining popularity.
Phase-5.1	**Purpose extends beyond Shareholder Value:** The **purpose** expands to *Larger* **Purpose** towards serving a common good beyond mere shareholder value; it influences the decisions being made day to day. Decisions and actions, once in line with *Larger* **Purpose**, remove all ambiguities and conflicts and enables people to perform with conviction and put in their best efforts. People find some meaning in the work they do and find it fulfilling.

Phase-5.2	**Serving larger common good, making an impact in the domain the organisation operates**: The organisation looks to make some meaningful impact on the people it touches. Become a place with highly-energetic and engaged people. Be an organisation that renews itself with proactive people, knowing exactly what to do without being told. Create a value-based culture without contradictions and conflicts. Become an admired organisation for stakeholders and gain respect from society.
VALUES	
Phase	**Explanation**
Phase-1	**Dormant**: At the initial stages, the organisation has other concerns, which overshadow the need for adopting values in the operations.
Phase-2.1	**Not articulated**: At this stage of evolution, though the leadership has values in mind, it does not get much attention and, generally, values are not articulated or documented. Not considered as a priority, as other business objectives are in focus.
Phase-2.2	**Followed in isolated cases**: At this stage, in a few isolated instances, values like ethics or integrity come into play in the conduct of day-to-day operations. Decisions and actions are dictated by business concerns and, many times, corners are cut to get quick results, and values, many times, are compromised.

Phase-3.1	**Inconsistency in following**: The values of the top leadership have an impact on the decisions and the chosen paths. The people in the organisation have to accept it unquestioningly. The leadership's values are only in the mind and not articulated clearly. Consequently, there is inconsistency in abiding and following the values.
Phase-3.2	**Desire to be ethical**: There is a desire in the leadership's mind to be ethical in all business dealings. The other values like basic human values may not come into play unless there is a strong value base and commitment of the leadership. The leadership's style leaves a big impact on the culture of the developing organisation.
Phase-4.1	**Fully compliant to laws and regulations**: With so much focus on proper governance of the organisations today, understanding and following the rules governing business becomes imperative. The values, like not cheating, not bribing, disclosing correct data and information, not accepting wrongdoing, complying with business rules and regulations and complying with the same in actions has to become a practice within the organisations at this stage of evolution.

Phase-4.2	**Human Values articulated – inconsistency in following**: These are values that influence human interactions, through processes and behaviour. Some of the basic human values are honesty, integrity, respect and care. If these become a part of the operating culture or not depends on the **paradigm** of the leadership. In most organisations, the adoption of such "best practices" is inconsistent.
Phase-5	**Ethics, Human and dharmic values enshrined in operating values**: Strong adherence to business ethics supported by adoption of human values and a set of dharmic values constitute the *Holistic* Values. These are often combined together as operating values or codes of conduct, which govern all strategies and actions.

LEADERSHIP PARADIGM ON PEOPLE	
Phase	**Explanation**
Phase-1.1	**Looks for basic competence**: Looks for people, basic/minimum qualifications and an ability to understand and do what is required for the job.
Phase-1.2	**Just a means (resource)**: Looks at a person who is employed as a means or a resource. Not treated as a human being deserving acknowledgement and respect. Hire and fire approach with people.

Phase-2	**Looks for functional competency fit**: Looks for competency to execute the job. Also looks at the ability to work. Still not considered a human being deserving acknowledgement and respect. Hire and fire approach persists. Behavioural aspects not considered.
Phase-3.1	**Looks for functional and behavioural competency:** Recognises the need to train and develop people with the ability to perform better in their jobs. Training is done to perform better. The attitude towards people becomes more and more important.
Phase-3.2	**Willing to train and develop skills**: Leader looks for behavioural competence (attitude) apart from functional skills. Recognises the need to not only train but also "develop" people.
Phase-4.1	**Culture fit overrides "competence fit"**: Starts treating people not just as a resource. Leadership has the sensitivity that people need to be cared for and getting them engaged becomes necessary. Policies are adapted to address this aspect.
Phase-4.2	**Cares for people**: Starts to create an organisation where people are cared for. The view of people becomes a little more holistic—to look at them as human beings that need to be cared for. Policies are adapted to improve people "satisfaction".

Phase-4.3	**Develop and mentor people:** While competence fit is important, culture fits override this. Hire for attitude and develop competence. Accepts that people need to be mentored, and a leadership pipeline is created. Accepts responsibility for developing people as a whole.
Phase-4.4	**Rule bound:** Empathy missing in many situations. Despite all this, the organisation tends to become rule bound. Unless the leadership's orientation towards people has a strong element of empathy, the expectations of people cannot be fully met. Disengagement of people becomes a challenge.
Phase-5.1	**Empowering people to contribute to purpose:** The leader provides the environment for people to experiment, fail, work without fear, freely contribute thoughts and ideas for the organisation to grow. The leader should facilitate people working in consonance with purpose. Should be able to filter out people who are not aligned to purpose and who operate only for personal gain.
Phase-5.2	**Empathetic. Feels responsible for enabling people to develop to full potential:** The leader recognises the primacy of people and nurtures them to full potential. Is fully conscious that developing people is one of his/her core responsibilities and cannot be left to "Human Resources Department". This becomes a key strength of the organisation.

Phase-5.3	Fuelling a culture of selfless contribution and service and providing *Psychic Safety*: The leadership demonstrates a spirit of selflessness. Serving common good or humanity in general, in line with purpose, overrides personal gains. The leader constantly re-energises people to rise to their full potential. Provides a safety net for people to try new things and removes fear of failure, thereby nurturing innovation.
LEADERSHIP BUSINESS PARADIGM	
Phase	**Explanation**
Phase-1	**Get things done:** Few result-oriented objectives, leader finds ways to do it, what a leader says holds sway.
Phase-2	**Pushing growths:** Understands various factors that need to be managed. Understands the parameters governing growth and directs effort.
Phase-3.1	**Operational efficiency:** Focus shifts to operating efficiencies and processes become important.
Phase-3.2	**Customer orientation**: Recognises that customer is the key for the business. Directs operations towards meeting customer's expectations.
Phase-4	**Business Visionary**: Understands the importance to look and plan ahead. Has a long-term perspective. Creates and deploys vision across the organisation. Organisation objectives become clearer to people.

Phase-5.1	**Earning the respect of all stakeholders, including society at large**: The paradigm is to conduct the business in such a manner so that it not only satisfies all the stakeholders but also earns their respect. The leadership's role model behaviour has an impact on all stakeholders— people, customers, suppliers, business partners and society at large.
Phase-5.2	**Impact beyond business**: Business paradigm looks beyond the confines of business and seeks alignment to purpose. Looks for opportunities to make an IMPACT.

www.ingramcontent.com/pod-product-compliance
Lightning Source LLC
Chambersburg PA
CBHW030622220526
45463CB00004B/1385